Cookie Jar
Cookbook

Produced by the staff of *Farm Wife News*

Edited by Annette Gohlke, Food Editor

Illustrations by Peggy Bjorkman

Associate Artist, Janet Sanford

Production: Sally Radtke, Brenda Gordon

ISBN 0-89821-016-X
Reiman Publications, Inc.
P.O. Box 643
Milwaukee, Wisconsin 53201

SECOND PRINTING

From Our Kitchen

Dear Friends of Farm Wife News:

Here is your Cookie Jar Cookbook, the fourth in our series of specialized cookbooks . . . fresh from the recipe-testing kitchen of Farm Wife News.

As all of you know, it's a near disaster when that cookie jar is empty in any farm home! That was evidenced by the tremendous response to our "Rural Recipe Roundup" cookie contest—farm "Moms" from all over the nation told us cookies disappear faster than any other dessert, and it's practically a must to stop everything else when that popular jar needs refilling!

Here's plenty of help next time that "crisis" occurs at your home. Within the pages of this Cookie Jar Cookbook you will find more than 100 of the best cookie recipes (we received well over a thousand) from farm wives. Each of these are "farm-kitchen-tested" cookie recipes—they're already proven favorites of farm kids and husbands.

Our first three cookbooks in this series—Pies Aplenty, Cakes Aplenty and Vegetable Bounty—have been well received. Many Farm Wife News readers have purchased all three for their personal files, and as gifts for friends as well.

This fourth book should be another treasured recipe book, since it will help solve the "cookie jar crisis" in many farm homes. Again, we sincerely thank all the farm and ranch wives who have shared their top recipes with us . . . and with you.

Here's wishing you good cooking . . . and good cookies!

Annette Gohlke

FWN Food Editor

Contents

Butter Cookies

SUGAR COOKIES

1 cup white sugar
1 cup powdered sugar
1 cup butter
2 eggs
1 cup vegetable oil

1 teaspoon vanilla
1 teaspoon salt
1 teaspoon baking soda
1 teaspoon cream of tartar
4 cups plus 2 tablespoons flour

Cream sugars and butter. Add eggs, then oil and vanilla. Beat until fluffy. Combine dry ingredients and add gradually to creamed mixture. Chill dough for about 4 hours. Roll into 1-in. balls, place on ungreased cookie sheet and flatten with bottom of a glass dipped in sugar. Bake at 375° for 8 to 10 minutes or until lightly browned. Note: This dough may be rolled for cut-out cookies.

Mrs. Jerry Hastings, Britton, South Dakota

GOLDEN SUGAR COOKIES

1 cup butter	2-1/2 cups flour
2 cups sugar	1 teaspoon baking soda
1/2 teaspoon vanilla	1/4 teaspoon salt
1/2 teaspoon lemon extract	1 teaspoon cream of tartar
3 egg yolks	

Cream butter, sugar and flavorings together until fluffy. Add egg yolks, one at a time, beating well after each addition. Combine dry ingredients, gradually add to creamed mixture. Roll into 1-in. balls, place on ungreased cookie sheet. Bake at 350° for 10 minutes or until golden. Sprinkle with sugar as soon as removed from oven.

Mrs. Leonard Hartman, Kokomo, Indiana

SOUR CREAM COOKIES

1 cup butter or margarine	1 cup dairy sour cream
1-3/4 cup sugar	1 teaspoon baking soda
2 eggs	2 teaspoons baking powder
1/2 teaspoon salt	4 cups flour
2 teaspoons vanilla	

Cream butter and sugar. Add eggs, salt and vanilla, beat until creamy. Combine dry ingredients and add alternately with the sour cream to the creamed mixture. Drop by teaspoonfuls onto lightly greased cookie sheet. Decorate as desired. Bake at 350° about 15 minutes. **Variations:** Add 1/2 cup more flour, chill dough then roll out for cutout cookies: Add chocolate chips, raisins or nuts:

Mrs. Jane Holtz, Sumner, Iowa

MEXICAN WEDDING COOKIES

1 cup butter	1/4 teaspoon salt
1/2 confectioners sugar	1 teaspoon vanilla
2 cups flour	

Cream butter, add sugar; blend until smooth. Add remaining ingredients. Mixture will be stiff. Break off pieces with the tip of a teaspoon. Place on cookie sheet. Bake at 400° for 10 to 12 minutes. Roll in confectioners sugar.

Mrs. C. E. Saylor, Beardstown, Illinois

OLD-TIME CINNAMON JUMBLES

1/2 cup shortening (part butter)	1 teaspoon vanilla
1 cup sugar	2 cups flour
1 egg	1/2 teaspoon baking soda
3/4 cup buttermilk	1/2 teaspoon salt

Cream shortening, sugar and egg. Stir in buttermilk and vanilla. Combine flour, soda and salt, add to batter. Chill dough. Drop by teaspoonfuls onto greased cookie sheets. Sprinkle with mixture of sugar and cinnamon (1/4 cup sugar and 1 teaspoon cinnamon). Bake at 400° for 8 to 10 minutes. Yield: 4 dozen.

Mrs. Herbert Besthorn, Claflin, Kansas

VANILLA SUGAR COOKIES

1 cup butter	2 eggs
1 cup shortening	4 cups flour
1 cup granulated sugar	1 teaspoon baking soda
1 cup confectioners sugar	1 teaspoon cream of tartar
2 teaspoon vanilla	1/2 teaspoon salt

Cream butter, shortening, sugars and vanilla until fluffy. Add eggs, one at a time, beating well after each. Combine dry ingredients, add gradually to creamed mixture. Roll into 1-in. balls, then roll in granulated sugar. Place on lightly greased cookie sheet. Bake at 375° for 8 to 10 minutes.

Mrs. Kathryn Witte, Richmond, Indiana

MELTING MOMENTS

1 cup butter	3/4 cup cornstarch
1/3 cup confectioners sugar	1 cup flour
1 teaspoon vanilla	

Cream butter, sugar and vanilla. Combine cornstarch and flour, stir into creamed mixture. Drop by teaspoonfuls onto cookie sheet. Bake at 350° for 12 to 14 minutes. Roll in confectioners sugar or frost, if desired. Fancy cookies may be made by placing dough into a pastry bag using a large decorator tip.

Mrs. Leonard Hartman, Kokomo, Indiana

Butterscotch Cookies

BUTTERSCOTCH ROLLED COOKIES

1 cup butter
1 cup brown sugar
1 egg
3 cups flour

2 tablespoons cream
1 cup butterscotch chips, melted
1 teaspoon vanilla

Cream butter and sugar, add egg, cream, vanilla and melted chips. Blend well. Stir in flour. Chill dough for easier handling. Roll 1/3 of dough at a time. Cut into squares or fancy shapes. Bake at 400° for 5 to 7 minutes. Cool and frost. **Baker's Frosting:** 1 cup powdered sugar, 1 egg white, 2 tablespoons milk, 2 tablespoons cake flour, 1/2 cup vegetable shortening or butter, vanilla and salt. Beat the above ingredients with electric mixer until light and fluffy. Then add 1 cup more of confectioners sugar.

Mrs. Delbert Heuer, Fountain City, Wisconsin

9

BIRD NEST COOKIES

1 cup butter
1/2 cup brown sugar
2 egg yolks
1/2 teaspoon vanilla
2 cups flour

1/4 teaspoon salt
2 egg whites
1-1/4 cup nuts, finely chopped
Icing, jam, jelly, or maraschino
  cherries

Cream butter, sugar and egg yolks until creamy. Blend in vanilla, salt and flour. Shape into 1-in. balls. Dip into slightly beaten egg whites, then roll in nuts. Bake at 350° for 5 minutes. Remove from oven and with a thimble, or edge of teaspoon make an indentation in center of each cookie. Return to oven and bake 8 minutes more. Cool. Fill with colored icing, jam, jelly or cherry half.

Mrs. Warren Culver, Hanna City, Illinois

BEST EVER BUTTERSCOTCH COOKIES

1 cup evaporated milk
1 tablespoon vinegar
1/2 cup butter
1-1/2 cup brown sugar
2 eggs
1 teaspoon vanilla

2-1/2 cups flour
1 teaspoon baking soda
1/2 teaspoon baking powder
1/2 teaspoon salt
2/3 cup nuts, chopped
Brown Butter Frosting

Mix milk and vinegar, set aside to sour. Cream butter, sugar, eggs and vanilla until fluffy. Add combined dry ingredients alternately with milk to creamed mixture, stirring well after each addition. Stir in nuts. Drop by teaspoonfuls onto greased cookie sheet. Bake at 350° 10 to 12 minutes. Frost with **Brown Butter Frosting:** Melt 1/2 cup butter until golden, beat in 2 cups confectioners sugar and 2 to 4 tablespoons hot water until spreadable. Yield: 8 dozen. Note: 1 cup dairy sour cream or buttermilk may be substituted for evaporated milk and vinegar.

Mrs. Gideon L. Yoder, Belleville, Pennsylvania

CARAMEL DELIGHTS

3/4 cup butter
3/4 cup powdered sugar
1 teaspoon vanilla

Caramel Topping:
28 light candy caramels
1/4 cup evaporated milk
1/4 cup butter

Chocolate icing:
1/2 cup chocolate chips
3 tablespoons evaporated milk
1 tablespoon butter

1/4 teaspoon salt
2 tablespoons evaporated milk
2 cups flour

1 cup powdered sugar
1 cup pecans, finely chopped

1/2 teaspoon vanilla
1/4 cup powdered sugar

Preheat oven to 350°. Cream butter, add sugar, blend in vanilla, salt and milk. Gradually stir in the flour. Roll dough 1/8-in. thick on floured surface. Cut into 1 x 2-in. rectangles or 1-in. squares. Place on ungreased cookie sheet and bake for 12 to 15 minutes. **Caramel topping:** Melt caramels with milk and butter over low heat. Stir occasionally. Mix in sugar and pecans. Spread filling over baked cookies. **Chocolate icing:** Melt chocolate chips with milk and butter over low heat. Blend in vanilla and sugar. Cool. Top each cookie with a small amount of icing.

Marla Wilkins, Tingley, Iowa

SAINT NICK COOKIES

1 cup shortening
1/2 cup butter
1 cup brown sugar
1 cup white sugar
1/2 cup evaporated milk
4 teaspoons cinnamon

1 teaspoon cloves
1 teaspoon nutmeg
1 teaspoon salt
1 teaspoon baking soda
4 cups flour
1/2 cup slivered almonds

Cream shortening, butter and sugars. Add milk, blend well. Stir in dry ingredients, then nuts. Roll into logs about 1-1/2-in. in diameter. Wrap and refrigerate overnight. Cut into slices about 1/4-in. thick. Bake at 275° about 35 minutes.

Mrs. Ron Vande Voort, Sully, Iowa

MAPLE BUTTER BALLS

2 cups flour
2 tablespoons sugar
2 teaspoons baking powder
1/4 teaspoon salt
1 cup butter

1 8-ounce package cream cheese
2 eggs
1 cup sugar
1 teaspoon maple flavoring

Combine flour, sugar, baking powder and salt. Cream butter and cream cheese. Add eggs, beat well. Stir in flour. Chill dough 2 hours. Shape into balls, roll in sugar mixed with the teaspoon of maple flavoring. Bake on ungreased cookie sheet at 325° for 15 minutes. Yield: 5 dozen.

Mrs. August Herke, Howard, South Dakota

SOFT COOKIES: *To keep cookies soft in cookie jar, tuck in a crust of bread.*

Mrs. Ruth J. Higgins, Knowlesville, New York

THIMBLE SEALER: *When making filled cookies, use a thimble on your finger to press and seal edges of cookie. Makes a pretty scalloped edge, and is quick and easy.*

Mrs. W. C. Jervis, Somerville, Massachusetts

MELON BALLS: *To shape 1-in. balls when making cookies, use a melon ball cutter. Scoop out dough and you have a round ball.*

Mrs. Violet Ford, Portland, Oregon

COOKIE DESIGNS: *Give rolled cookies a fancy raised design by pressing the different knives of your food chopper into tops of cookies before baking. Add a raisin or pecan in the center.*

Mrs. Elizabeth Newton, Wyoming, Michigan

Cheese Cookies

LEMON COTTAGE CHEESE COOKIES

1/2 cup butter
1-1/2 cup sugar
2 eggs, beaten
2-1/2 teaspoons lemon juice
2 teaspoons lemon peel, grated

1 cup cottage cheese, sieved
2-1/2 cups flour
1/2 teaspoon salt
1 teaspoon baking powder

Cream butter, sugar and eggs until fluffy. Add juice and peel. Add cottage cheese, beat until smooth. Combine dry ingredients, add to creamed mixture. Drop by teaspoonfuls onto greased cookie sheet. Bake at 400° 10 to 15 minutes.

Nancy Hughes, Thorp, Wisconsin

CRULLERS

1 pound butter
1 pound cottage cheese

4 cups flour
Pinch salt

Filling:
2 pounds dates
1/2 cup water
1/2 cup sugar

1/2 cup walnuts, chopped
1/4 cup butter

Combine filling ingredients in saucepan and cook until thickened. Set aside to cool. Cream butter and cottage cheese; stir in flour and salt. Knead until blended. Shape into walnut size balls. Chill overnight. To bake, flatten balls, spread with filling. Roll up jelly roll fashion. Place seam side down on greased cookie sheet. Bake at 325° for 45 minutes or until brown. Roll in powdered sugar.

LeeAnn Smucker, Harrisburg, Oregon

CREAM CHEESE DAINTIES

6 ounces cream cheese
1 cup butter
1 cup sugar
1/2 teaspoon almond extract

1/2 teaspoon salt
2 cups flour
4 teaspoons baking powder
3 cups corn flakes, crushed

Cream cheese, butter and sugar, add almond extract. Combine salt, flour and baking powder, gradually add to creamed mixture. Mix well. Chill dough about 1 hour. Shape into small balls. Roll into corn flake crumbs. Place on ungreased cookie sheet, top with candied cherry slice. Bake at 350° 12 to 15 minutes. Yield: 6 dozen.

Sharon Manns, Alton, Illinois

CHEESE CRUNCHES

1/2 pound sharp Cheddar
cheese, grated
1/2 pound butter

2 cups flour
2-1/2 cups Rice
Krispie cereal

Mix cheese and butter. Blend in flour, then cereal. Form into balls and flatten on cookie sheet. Bake at 350° for 15 minutes. Yield: 70 cookies.

Audrey Rohrer, Lancaster, Pennsylvania

CHEDDAR NUT COOKIES

1/2 cup butter	3 cups flour
1 cup brown sugar	1/2 teaspoon baking soda
1/2 cup white sugar	1 teaspoon salt
2 eggs	1 cup salted Spanish peanuts
1 teaspoon vanilla	1 cup grated sharp
1 cup evaporated milk	Cheddar cheese

Cream butter, sugars, egg and vanilla. Combine dry ingredients and add alternately with milk. Stir in peanuts and cheese. Drop by teaspoonfuls onto greased cookie sheet. Bake at 350° about 10 minutes. Yield: 60 cookies. Frost if desired with **Caramel Frosting**: 1/2 cup butter, 1 cup brown sugar, 1/4 cup evaporated milk, 2 cups confectioners sugar. Melt butter, stir in brown sugar. Heat to boiling, stirring constantly. Boil and stir over low heat for 2 minutes. Add milk and return to boil. Cool to lukewarm. Stir in confectioners sugar to spreading consistency.

Mrs. Allen Adams, Caroline, Wisconsin

PIZZA CUTTER: *Cut bar cookies or rolled cookies with a pizza cutter. It's quick and easy.*

Mrs. H. J. Sherrer, Bay City, Texas

EXTRA COOKIE SHEETS: *Drop cookies onto foil the same size as your cookie sheets. When first batch is baked, just remove foil from pan to cool on wire rack and replace with another cookie-filled foil sheet.*

Mrs. Violet Ford, Portland, Oregon

COOKIE TIME: *In the wintertime, most of us do a lot of cookie baking. Here is a little tip for sugar cookies. Add 1/2 to 1 tablespoon of grated orange peel to your dough. Gives a "zip" to an otherwise "flat" cookie.*

Mrs. Bob Roach, Faucett, Missouri

Chocolate Cookies

CHOCOLATE DOLLARS

2-1/2 cups flour
1-1/2 teaspoon baking powder
1/4 teaspoon salt
1/2 teaspoon cinnamon
1 egg, slightly beaten
1 cup sugar

1/2 cup shortening
2 tablespoons milk
2 ounces unsweetened
chocolate, melted
1/2 cup nuts
1 teaspoon vanilla

Combine dry ingredients. Cream egg, sugar, shortening, milk and chocolate. Stir in dry ingredients, then nuts. Shape dough into rolls, wrap and chill thoroughly. Slice and bake at 400° on ungreased cookie sheet for 8 minutes. Yield: 4 dozen.

Mrs. Herbert Besthorn, Claflin, Kansas

CUCKOO COOKIES

1-3/4 cup flour
1/2 teaspoon baking soda
1/2 teaspoon salt
1/2 cup cocoa
1/2 cup shortening
1 cup sugar

1 egg
1/2 cup milk
1 teaspoon vanilla
1/2 cup walnuts, chopped
24 large marshmallows,
cut in halves

Glaze:
1/2 cup cocoa
1-1/2 cup confectioners
sugar

3 tablespoons hot strong
coffee
1/2 cup butter, melted

Combine flour, soda, salt and cocoa. Cream shortening and sugar, beat in egg. Add flour alternately with milk, beating well. Add vanilla and nuts. Drop by teaspoonfuls onto greased cookie sheet. Bake at 350° 8 minutes. Top each cookie with a marshmallow half, pressing gently onto partially baked cookie. Return to oven and bake 4 minutes more. Cool and glaze. Yield: 4 dozen.

Ina McKern, Rice, Washington

CHOCOLATE DROP COOKIES

1 cup shortening
4 ounces unsweetened chocolate
2 cups brown sugar
1 cup sour or buttermilk
2 eggs
1 teaspoon baking soda

1 teaspoon baking powder
1/4 teaspoon salt
3 cups flour
1 teaspoon vanilla
1 cup nuts
1 cup chocolate chips, optional

Melt shortening and chocolate. Cool slightly. Add sugar, milk and eggs; beat well. Combine dry ingredients, stir into above mixture. Add vanilla, nuts and chocolate chips, if desired. Drop by teaspoonfuls onto greased cookie sheet. Bake at 350° for 10 to 12 minutes. Frost if desired with **Chocolate Glaze:** Reserve 1/2 square of melted chocolate from cookie recipe above. Add 2 tablespoons melted butter. Stir in 1 cup powdered sugar, 1 tablespoon hot water and 1/2 teaspoon vanilla.

Mrs. Francis J. Mootz, Bellevue, Iowa

CHOCOLATE WEDDING CAKES

1-1/4 cup butter
  2/3 cup confectioners sugar
  2 teaspoons vanilla
  2 cups flour

1/2 cup cocoa
1/2 teaspoon salt
  2 cups walnuts,
    chopped fine

Cream butter, sugar and vanilla. Combine dry ingredients, stir into creamed mixture, blending well. Blend in nuts. Chill dough for at least 1 hour. Roll into 1-in. balls. Bake on ungreased cookie sheet at 350° for 18 to 20 minutes, or until done. Roll in confectioners sugar.

Lynn Walker, Joliet, Illinois

CHOCOLATE MALTED COOKIES

1-1/4 cup flour
  1 cup chocolate malted powder
  1 teaspoon baking powder
  1/4 teaspoon salt
  1/2 cup softened butter

1 cup brown sugar
1 egg
1 teaspoon vanilla
1/4 cup evaporated milk
1 cup nuts, chopped

Combine dry ingredients. Cream butter, sugar, egg and vanilla. Beat in milk. Stir in dry ingredients, add nuts. Refrigerate for 1 hour. Drop by teaspoonfuls onto greased cookie sheet. Bake at 350° for 10 to 12 minutes. Yield: 4 dozen.

Mrs. Evonne Jennett, Blockton, Iowa

CHOCOLATE MACROONS

4 eggs, separated
1 pound confectioners sugar
2 tablespoons water
1/2 cup ground or slivered almonds

1 bar German sweet chocolate, grated
1 teaspoon baking powder
2-1/2 cups flour

Beat yolks until light lemon color and fluffy. Add confectioners sugar and water; blend. Combine flour and baking powder, add to above mixture in several portions. Beat whites until soft peaks form (not stiff). Fold into batter along with chocolate. Chill for about 1/2 hour before dropping by teaspoonfuls onto greased cookie sheet. Bake at 350° 12 to 15 minutes. These cookies spread, do not place dough too close together.

Mrs. Floyd R. Collison, Pigeon, Michigan

CHOCOLATE SANDWICHES

1 cup soft butter
2 cups sugar
2 eggs
1 teaspoon vanilla
2 cups milk

4 cups flour
1 teaspoon baking powder
3 teaspoons baking soda
1 teaspoon salt
1 cup cocoa

Marshmallow Filling:
3/4 cup white shortening (Crisco)
4 cups confectioners sugar
3 to 4 tablespoons milk

1 pint jar marshmallow creme
1 teaspoon vanilla

Cream butter, sugar, eggs and vanilla until fluffy. Combine dry ingredients and add alternately to creamed mixture with milk. Drop by teaspoonfuls onto greased cookie sheet. Bake at 400° about 7 minutes. Cool. **Filling:** Cream shortening and 2 cups sugar, add milk and beat until fluffy. Fold in marshmallow creme, vanilla and remaining 2 cups sugar, beat well. Assemble sandwich cookie by placing marshmallow filling between 2 cookies.

Mrs. Joseph J. Friederick, Lancaster, Wisconsin

CHOCOLATE COCONUT MERINGUE COOKIES

6 ounces semi-sweet chocolate chips
3 egg whites
1/8 teaspoon salt

1 cup confectioners sugar
1-1/3 cup flaked coconut
3/4 cup graham cracker crumbs
1/2 teaspoon vanilla

Preheat oven to 325°. Melt chocolate over hot water. Beat egg whites and salt until foamy. Add sugar, 2 tablespoons at a time, beating thoroughly after each addition. Continue beating until mixture forms stiff peaks. Fold in chocolate and remaining ingredients. Drop by teaspoonfuls onto greased cookie sheets and bake about 11 minutes. Yield: 3-1/2 dozen cookies.

Mrs. Gilbert Anderson, Haxtun, Colorado

Chocolate Chip Cookies

SNOWBALL DAINTIES

3/4 cup butter, softened
1/3 cup sugar
  1 tablespoon water
  1 teaspoon vanilla
  2 cups flour
1/8 teaspoon salt

  6 ounces mint flavored
    chocolate chips
1/2 cup candied red cherries,
    chopped
  1 cup pecans, chopped

Cream butter, sugar, water, and vanilla. Add remaining ingredients, except nuts, blending well. Chill dough about 1 hour. Shape into 1-in. balls, roll in nuts. Place on ungreased cookie sheet. Bake at 300° for 30 minutes. Roll in confectioners sugar while still warm, if desired. Yield: 3 dozen.

Mrs. Gene Wehrbein, Louisville, Nebraska

CHOCOLATE YUMMIES

1 small box chocolate pudding
   mix (not instant)
2 cups Bisquick mix
1/2 cup sugar
1 egg, slightly beaten

1/3 cup milk
1/4 cup butter, melted
1 teaspoon vanilla
1-1/3 cup coconut, optional
1 cup chocolate chips, optional

Combine pudding mix, Bisquick and sugar. Beat in next 4 ingredients. Stir in coconut or chocolate chips, or one half of each amount. Drop onto ungreased cookie sheet. Bake at 350° for 10 to 12 minutes. Vary this recipe using other pudding flavors.

Mrs. Leonard Hartman, Kokomo, Indiana

M&M CANDY COOKIES

1 cup shortening
1 cup brown sugar
1/2 cup white sugar
2 eggs
1-1/2 teaspoon vanilla

2-1/4 cups flour
1 teaspoon baking soda
1 teaspoon salt
1-1/2 cup M&M chocolate
   candy

Cream shortening, sugars, eggs and vanilla until fluffy. Stir in remaining ingredients. Drop by teaspoonfuls onto cookie sheet. Bake at 375° 8 to 10 minutes.

Mrs. Alton A. Bauer, Herreid, South Dakota

CHOCOLATE CHIP COOKIES

1 cup brown sugar
1 cup white sugar
1 cup salad oil
1 cup shortening (part butter)
2 eggs
2 teaspoons vanilla

4 cups flour
2 teaspoons baking soda
4 teaspoons cream of tartar
1 teaspoon salt
1 cup chocolate chips
   (miniature)

Combine ingredients, mixing well. Drop by teaspoonfuls onto cookie sheet. Bake at 350° 10 to 12 minutes.

Mrs. Cordell Wubbin, Raymond, Minnesota

PHILLY CHIPPERS

1 cup butter
8 ounces cream cheese
3/4 cup granulated sugar
3/4 cup brown sugar
1 egg
1 teaspoon vanilla

2-1/2 cups flour
1 teaspoon baking powder
1/2 teaspoon salt
12 ounces chocolate chips
1/2 cup nuts, chopped fine

Cream butter, cheese, sugars, egg and vanilla. Beat until fluffy. Combine dry ingredients, add to creamed mixture and stir until blended. Add chocolate chips and nuts. Drop by teaspoonfuls onto greased cookie sheet. Bake at 375° 15 to 18 minutes. Yield: 5 dozen.

Mrs. Ken Stoner, Lititz, Pennsylvania

BOHEMIAN COOKIES

1 cup butter
1-1/4 cup confectioners sugar
1 teaspoon vanilla
Dash salt

1-1/4 cup flour
6 ounces chocolate chips,
ground
1 cup walnuts, ground

Cream butter, sugar and vanilla until fluffy. Add salt and flour, stir until blended. Stir in ground chocolate and nuts. Drop by teaspoonfuls onto ungreased cookie sheet. Bake at *250°* for 40 minutes.

Mary Matulnik, Anderson, Indiana

CHOCOLATE SPRINKLES: *Use those leftover sprinkles from holiday baking by substituting them for chocolate chips in a cookie recipe. They're also delicious added to a mixture of peanut butter and honey for a sandwich spread. Spread on toast or crackers, then pop into oven to heat slightly.*

Mrs. Pat Lewis, Thayer, Kansas

Coconut Cookies

PERSIAN COOKIES

1 cup shortening
1 teaspoon salt
1 teaspoon vanilla
1-1/4 cup sugar
2 eggs, beaten
3 cups sifted flour
3 teaspoons baking powder

1/4 cup milk
1/3 cup dates
1/2 cup ground figs
1/3 cup candied pineapple
2 cups shredded coconut, cut fine
1/3 cup walnuts, chopped

Cream first 5 ingredients until fluffy. Stir in flour and baking powder. Add milk, blend well. Stir in remaining ingredients. Drop by teaspoonfuls onto greased cookie sheet. Flatten slightly. Bake at 350° 12 to 15 minutes. Note: Allow cookies to ripen for several weeks in covered container.

Mrs. Floyd R. Collison, Pigeon, Michigan

COCONUT CREAM CHEESE COOKIES

1 cup butter	1 egg
2 3-ounce packages cream cheese	2 tablespoons milk
1 cup sugar	2 cups flour
1/4 teaspoon salt	1/2 cup coconut
1 teaspoon vanilla	Walnut halves

Cream butter, cream cheese, sugar, salt, flavorings, egg and milk until fluffy. Stir in flour and coconut. Drop by teaspoonfuls onto ungreased cookie sheet. Top each cookie with walnut half. Bake at 325° for 20 minutes. Yield: 5 dozen.

Mrs. Blaine T. Myers, Dillsburg, Pennsylvania

CORN FLAKE COOKIES

8 egg whites	2 cups shredded coconut
2 cups granulated sugar	6 cups corn flakes
2 cups nuts, chopped	1 teaspoon vanilla

Beat egg whites until stiff, gradually add sugar, beating until sugar is well dissolved and meringue is stiff and glossy. Add vanilla. Gently fold in coconut, corn flakes and nuts. Drop by teaspoonfuls onto greased cookie sheet. Bake at 350° until slightly browned.

Mrs. Ivan Kahle, Norwood, Minnesota

JUBILEE JUMBLES

1/2 cup shortening	2-3/4 cups flour
1 cup brown sugar	1/2 teaspoon baking soda
1/2 cup white sugar	1 teaspoon salt
2 eggs	1 cup pecans, chopped
1 cup evaporated milk	1 cup coconut
1 teaspoon vanilla	

Cream shortening, sugars and eggs until fluffy. Stir in milk and vanilla; then dry ingredients. Drop by teaspoonfuls onto cookie sheet. Bake at 375° 10 minutes. Frost with **Burnt Butter Glaze:** Heat 2 tablespoons butter until golden. Beat in 2 cups confectioners sugar and 1/4 cup undiluted evaporated milk.

Mrs. Harold Hermsen, New Vienna, Iowa

COFFEE WALNUT HAYSTACKS

1 egg
1 egg yolk
3/4 cup brown sugar
1 tablespoon flour
1 tablespoon instant coffee powder

2 teaspoons soft butter
2 cups walnuts, coarsely broken
1-1/2 cups flaked coconut
1 cup dates, finely cut

Beat egg and yolk until light. Beat in sugar, then flour, coffee powder and butter. Add walnuts, coconut and dates, stirring until well blended. Drop by teaspoonfuls onto greased cookie sheet. Bake at 300° 12 to 14 minutes. Allow cookies to cool about 3 minutes, before removing carefully to wire racks. Pinch cookies together gently when removing from cookie sheet. Yield: 3 dozen.

Mrs. Keith Wilson, DeSmet, Idaho

SPECIAL COCONUT MACAROONS

1/2 cup egg whites
1/2 cup sugar
1 teaspoon vanilla
1/2 cup flour

1/8 teaspoon salt
3/4 cup sugar
2-1/2 cups flaked coconut

Beat egg whites until soft peaks form. Gradually add 1/2 cup sugar, beating constantly until stiff and glossy. Add vanilla. Combine flour, salt and 3/4 cup sugar; add coconut. Fold into egg white meringue. Drop by rounded teaspoonfuls onto brown paper lined cookie sheet. Bake at 325° for 20 to 25 minutes. Remove cookies carefully. Cool. Note: For easy removal, place brown paper on wet towel for 2 minutes. Cookies may be decorated with colored sugar before baking; or, after baking, drizzle with chocolate glaze made with 1/3 cup semi-sweet chocolate chips melted with 1 tablespoon milk.

Mrs. Vernon E. Zickert, Deerfield, Wisconsin

SANTA'S WHISKERS

1 cup butter
1 cup sugar
2 tablespoons milk
1 teaspoon vanilla
2-1/2 cups flour

3/4 cup red and green candied
cherries, finely chopped
1/2 cup pecans, finely chopped
3/4 cup flaked coconut

Cream butter, sugar and milk; add vanilla. Stir in flour, cherries and nuts. Shape into 2 rolls about 2 in. in diameter. Roll in coconut, wrap and chill several hours or overnight. Slice, place on ungreased cookie sheet and bake at 375° for about 12 minutes. Yield: 5 dozen.

Mrs. Kenneth Clasen, Erie, Kansas

COCONUT CRISPIES

1 cup butter
1 cup sugar
1 egg
3 cups coconut

2-1/4 cups flour
1/2 teaspoon salt
1/2 teaspoon baking soda
Pecan halves

Cream butter, sugar and egg until fluffy. Add about 2 cups coconut and dry ingredients. Knead dough until smooth. Shape into 2 rolls about 1-1/2 in. in diameter. Roll in remaining coconut, wrap and chill. Slice, place on greased cookie sheet. Brush top of cookie with mixture of egg yolk and 1 tablespoon milk. Press pecan half onto each cookie. Bake at 325° 20 to 25 minutes. Yield: 5-6 dozen.

Mrs. William Brook, East Lansing, Michigan

COCONUT PASTEL COOKIES

1 cup butter
1/2 cup sugar
3-ounce package strawberry
flavored gelatin
2 eggs
1 teaspoon vanilla
1/2 teaspoon almond extract

2-3/4 cups flour
1 teaspoon baking soda
1/2 teaspoon salt
1/2 cup milk
1-1/3 cup coconut
Pink decorating sugar

Cream butter, sugar, gelatin, eggs and flavorings until fluffy. Stir in flour, baking powder and salt. Add milk, then coconut. Drop by teaspoonfuls onto ungreased cookie sheet, sprinkle cookies with decorating sugar. Bake at 350° for 10 minutes. Yield: 5 dozen.

Mrs. LaVerne Weber, Richland, Iowa

MOUNT SHASTA COOKIES

1/2 cup shortening
1 teaspoon vanilla
1/2 cup sugar
1/2 cup brown sugar
2 egg yolks
3 tablespoons milk

1-1/2 cup flour
1/2 teaspoon salt
1 cup walnuts, chopped
2 egg whites
1/2 cup sugar
1 cup moist coconut

Cream shortening, vanilla 1/2 cup granulated sugar, brown sugar, and egg yolks until creamy. Add milk, mix well. Stir in flour and salt. Fold in nuts. Drop by teaspoonfuls onto ungreased cookie sheet. Flatten slightly. Beat the egg whites until frothy. Add the 1/2 cup sugar gradually, beating well after each addition until stiff peaks form. Fold in coconut. Top each cookie with a teaspoonful of coconut meringue. Bake at 375° 10 to 12 minutes or until meringue is lightly browned. Yield: 4 to 5 dozen.

Mrs. L. D. Catron, Caldwell, Texas

10 MINUTE MAGIC MACAROONS

2/3 cup Eagle brand sweetened
   condensed milk
3 cups shredded coconut

1 teaspoon vanilla
3/4 teaspoon almond extract

Combine ingredients. Drop by teaspoonfuls onto greased cookie sheet. Bake at 350° 8 to 10 minutes, until delicately browned. Yield: 30 cookies.

Mrs. Irene Johnson, Cedar Falls, Iowa

HOLIDAY JEWELS

4-ounce jar red
   maraschino cherries
4-ounce jar green
   maraschino cherries
1 cup coconut

4 cups cornflakes
6 tablespoons flour
14-ounce can Eagle brand
   sweetened condensed milk
1 teaspoon vanilla

Drain well and chop cherries. Combine dry ingredients, add cherries, milk and vanilla, mix well. Drop by teaspoonfuls onto well greased cookie sheet. Bake at 350° 10 to 12 minutes.

Mrs. Frank J. Vrba, Schuyler, Nebraska

TOASTED COCONUT COOKIES

2 cups flaked coconut
1/2 cup Eagle brand sweetened
condensed milk
1/4 cup corn syrup (dark or light)
3 tablespoons brown sugar

2 tablespoons soft butter
1/8 teaspoon salt
1 teaspoon vanilla
1/2 cup Quaker's instant oatmeal

Preheat oven to 350°. Sprinkle coconut onto lightly greased cookie sheet. Toast for 10 to 12 minutes, stirring occasionally until lightly browned. Cool. Combine remaining ingredients, stir in coconut. Drop by teaspoonfuls onto greased cookie sheet, bake at 350° 12 to 15 minutes. Cookie may be frosted with melted almond bark, chocolate or butterscotch chips.

Mrs. Otto Fahning, Wells, Minnesota

SOUR CREAM COOKIES WITH COCONUT

1/2 cup butter
3/4 cup brown sugar
1 egg + 1 egg yolk
3/4 cup flour
1/2 teaspoon baking soda

1/2 teaspoon salt
1/2 cup sour cream
1/2 teaspoon vanilla
1/2 cup nuts, finely chopped

Icing:
1-1/4 cup confectioners sugar
2 tablespoons butter
2 tablespoons milk

1/2 teaspoon vanilla
Grated coconut

Cream butter, sugar and egg, plus yolk. Add flour, baking soda and salt. Stir in sour cream and vanilla, then nuts. Drop by teaspoonfuls onto greased cookie sheet. Bake at 375° for 12 to 14 minutes. Cool, frost with Icing, then sprinkle top of cookie with coconut.

Mrs. Frank Graybill, Hershey, Pennsylvania

BUTTERSCOTCH COCONUT COOKIES

1 cup butter
1 cup granulated sugar
1/2 cup brown sugar
2 eggs
2-1/4 cups flour
1 teaspoon salt

1 teaspoon baking soda
1/2 teaspoon hot water
6 ounces butterscotch morsels
1 cup flaked coconut
Chopped nuts, optional

Preheat oven to 375°. Cream butter and sugars, add eggs and beat until light and fluffy. Add flour, salt and soda, blend well. Add hot water. Fold in butterscotch morsels, coconut and nuts. Drop by small teaspoonfuls onto greased cookie sheets. Bake for 10 to 12 minutes. Yield: 4 to 5 dozen.

Mrs. Anna LaBarr, Penn Yan, New York

MERRY MACAROONS

2 eggs
3/4 cup sugar
1/3 cup flour
1/4 teaspoon baking powder
1/8 teaspoon salt

1 tablespoon soft butter
1 teaspoon vanilla
2-3/4 cups shredded coconut,
   firmly packed

Beat eggs until foamy. Slowly add sugar, beat until thick and lemon color, about 5 minutes. Fold in dry ingredients, then beat in butter, vanilla and coconut. Drop by teaspoonfuls onto foil-lined cookie sheet. Bake at 325° about 15 minutes, until browned around edges. Cool slightly, before removing from baking sheets. Yield: 2-1/2 dozen chewy, sweet cookies.

Mrs. Fae E. Martin, Selinsgrove, Pennsylvania

JUICE CAN COOKIE MOLD: *Refrigerate or freeze cookie dough in 6-ounce juice cans. Cut out both ends of can, fill with dough. When ready to bake cookies, just push dough out of can, slice and bake!*

Mrs. Naomi K. Gisick, Timken, Kansas

Fruit Cookies

ORANGE GLAZED PRUNE COOKIES

2 cups brown sugar
1 cup shortening
2 eggs
1/2 cup milk
3-1/2 cups flour
1 teaspoon baking soda

1/2 teaspoon salt
1 teaspoon baking powder
1 teaspoon cinnamon
2 cups prunes, cooked, chopped
1 cup walnuts, chopped
1 teaspoon vanilla

Cream sugar and shortening. Stir in eggs and milk. Combine dry ingredients and add to creamed mixture. Add prunes, nuts and vanilla. Drop by teaspoonfuls onto greased cookie sheet. Bake at 350° 15 to 20 minutes. Cool and frost with **Orange Glaze:** 3 cups confectioners sugar, grated rind of one orange and 4 tablespoons orange juice.

Mrs. Leonard B. Larson, Mabel, Minnesota

FRUIT COCKTAIL COOKIES

1 cup shortening
1 cup brown sugar
1/2 cup white sugar
3 eggs
2 teaspoons vanilla
1 teaspoon baking soda

1 teaspoon baking powder
1 teaspoon salt
4 cups flour
2 cups fruit cocktail,
  well drained
3/4 cup walnuts, chopped

Frosting:
6 tablespoons butter
3 cups powdered sugar

4 tablespoons hot water

Cream shortening, sugars, eggs and vanilla until fluffy. Combine dry ingredients, stir about 3 cups into creamed mixture. Add fruit and nuts, then stir in last cup of flour. Drop by large teaspoonfuls onto greased cookie sheet, bake at 350° for 10 minutes. Cool and frost. **Frosting:** Brown butter in heavy skillet, do not burn. Remove from heat, add sugar and hot water, 1 tablespoon at a time, beating until frosting is spreadable.

Mrs. Orpha Hilde, Chisago City, Minnesota

CRANBERRY COOKIES

1/2 cup butter
1 cup sugar
3/4 cup brown sugar
1/4 cup milk
2 teaspoons orange juice
1 egg
3 cups flour

1/4 teaspoon baking soda
1 teaspoon baking powder
1/2 teaspoon salt
1 cup nuts, chopped
2-1/2 cups cranberries,
  coarsely chopped
1 teaspoon vanilla

Cream butter and sugars. Add milk, juice and egg, beat well. Combine dry ingredients, stir into creamed mixture. Stir in nuts, cranberries and vanilla. Drop by teaspoonfuls onto greased cookie sheet. Bake at 375° 10 to 15 minutes.

Mrs. Richard L. Enders, Halifax, Pennsylvania

ORANGE REFRIGERATOR COOKIES

1 cup butter	3 cups flour
1-1/2 cup brown sugar	2 teaspoons baking powder
1 egg	1/2 teaspoon salt
2 tablespoons grated orange rind	1/4 teaspoon baking soda
2 tablespoons orange juice	1 cup walnuts, chopped

Cream butter and sugar. Add egg, rind and juice; beat until fluffy. Combine dry ingredients and nuts, stir into batter. Divide dough into 2 portions. Shape each portion into roll about 1-1/2 in. in diameter. Wrap and chill overnight. Slice 1/4 in. thick, place on ungreased cookie sheet. Bake at 400° for about 10 minutes. Yield: 4 dozen.

Mrs. Walter Kutz, Palmer, Nebraska

LEMONADE COOKIES

1 cup butter	1 teaspoon baking soda
1 cup sugar	1/2 cup frozen lemonade,
2 eggs	thawed, undiluted
3 cups flour	

Cream butter, sugar and eggs until fluffy. Combine flour and soda, add alternately with lemonade (undiluted) to creamed mixture. Drop by teaspoonfuls onto ungreased cookie sheet. Bake at 400° 8 minutes. Brush hot cookies lightly with lemonade concentrate. Sprinkle with sugar. Cool on wire rack. Yield: 4 dozen.

Mrs. E. R. Brown, Hutchinson, Kansas

APRICOT COOKIES

1/2 cup butter	1/4 cup sugar
3 ounces cream cheese	1-1/2 teaspoon baking powder
1/2 cup apricot preserves	1/4 teaspoon salt
1-1/4 cup flour	1/2 cup flaked coconut

Cream butter, cream cheese and preserves. Add remaining ingredients, blend well. Drop by teaspoonfuls onto ungreased cookie sheet. Bake at 350° 15 to 18 minutes.

Mrs. Gordon Fjestad, Fergus Falls, Minnesota

CHERRY POM POMS

3 tablespoons dry cherry
  flavored gelatin
1 small package instant
  vanilla pudding mix
1 cup flour
1/2 teaspoon baking powder
1/2 cup cooking oil
2 egg yolks

3 tablespoons milk
1/2 teaspoon almond extract
2 egg whites
1 tablespoon water
3/4 cup grated coconut
Chopped nuts or coconut
  for topping

Combine gelatin, pudding, flour and baking powder. Stir in the oil, egg yolks, milk and extract. Beat egg whites with 1 tablespoon water until foamy. Roll cookie mixture into balls, dip into beaten egg white, then in coconut or nuts. Bake at 350° for 15 minutes.

Mrs. Virgil James, Cumberland, Iowa

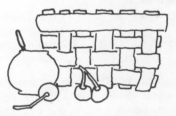

CHOCOLATE COVERED CHERRY COOKIES

1/2 cup softened butter
3/4 cup confectioners sugar sifted
1 tablespoon vanilla
1 ounce unsweetened
  chocolate, melted

1-1/2 cup flour
1/8 teaspoon salt
Maraschino cherries, well
  drained or candied cherries

Cream butter, sugar vanilla and chocolate. Blend in flour and salt. If dough is too dry, add a teaspoon or two of cream. Pinch off small amount of dough, pat it flat, then wrap around a cherry, sealing well. Place on ungreased cookie sheet and bake at 350° 12 to 15 minutes. When cool, frost with **Chocolate Icing:** 1 cup confectioners sugar, 1/4 cup cream, 1 teaspoon vanilla and 1 square unsweetened chocolate, melted. Yield: 20-25 cookies.

Mrs. Howard Boardman, Northfield, Vermont

DIABETIC APPLESAUCE COOKIES

1/2 cup butter
1 tablespoon artificial sweetener
1 cup unsweetened applesauce
1 egg
Dash salt
1-3/4 cup flour

1/2 teaspoon cinnamon
1/2 teaspoon cloves
1 teaspoon baking soda
1 cup bran cereal <u>or</u>
Grape Nuts cereal
1/4 cup nuts, chopped

Melt butter, add sweetener and applesauce. Add egg, beat well. Stir in combined dry ingredients. Fold in cereal and nuts. Drop by teaspoonfuls onto greased cookie sheet. Bake at 375° for 20 minutes.

Mrs. John Klaholz, Jr., Huron, Ohio

BANANA COOKIES

2-1/4 cups flour
1/2 teaspoon baking powder
1/2 teaspoon baking soda
1/2 teaspoon salt
1 teaspoon cinnamon
1 cup sugar

1/3 cup shortening
1 egg
1 cup banana pulp
1 teaspoon vanilla
1/2 cup nuts, chopped, optional

Combine first five ingredients. Cream sugar, shortening and egg until fluffy. Stir in banana and vanilla. Blend in dry ingredients. Drop by teaspoonfuls onto greased cookie sheet. Bake at 350° for 15 minutes. Frost cookie if desired.

Cathy Ireland, Belvidere, South Dakota

PUMPKIN COOKIES

1/2 cup shortening
1-1/4 cup brown sugar
2 eggs
1 teaspoon vanilla
1-1/2 cup pumpkin
2-1/2 cups flour

4 teaspoons baking powder
1/2 teaspoon salt
1/2 teaspoon cinnamon
1/2 teaspoon nutmeg
1 cup raisins
1 cup walnuts, chopped

Cream shortening, sugar, eggs and vanilla until fluffy. Stir in pumpkin. Stir in combined dry ingredients. Add raisins and nuts. Drop by teaspoonfuls onto greased cookie sheet. Bake at 375° for 15 minutes.

Mrs. Donald Martin, Hoyt, Kansas

LEMON COCONUT DAINTIES

3/4 cup butter
1/2 cup sugar
1 egg
1 teaspoon vanilla

1/2 teaspoon lemon extract
2 cups flour
1-1/2 cups flaked coconut

Cream butter, sugar, and egg until fluffy. Stir in remaining ingredients, blend well. Shape into a roll, wrap and refrigerate overnight. Slice thin and bake at 400° 8 to 10 minutes until edges are lightly browned. When cool, frost with **Lemon Butter Icing:** 1/4 cup butter, 2 cups confectioners sugar, 1 teaspoon grated lemon rind, 4 teaspoons lemon juice, 1/8 teaspoon salt and enough milk or cream to make spreadable. Put two cookies together as a sandwich.

Mrs. Francis Jewett, Ruthton, Minnesota

LEMON LASSIES

Filling:
2 eggs, slightly beaten
1/2 cup sugar
1 tablespoon lemon rind, grated

1/4 cup lemon juice
1 teaspoon salt
1 cup coconut

Cookie:
2-1/4 cups flour
1 teaspoon cinnamon
1/2 teaspoon baking soda
1/4 teaspoon salt

1/2 cup butter
1 cup sugar
1 egg
1/4 cup light molasses

Combine all the filling ingredients except coconut. Cook over low heat, stirring constantly until thick. Remove from heat and add coconut. Set aside to cool. Combine flour, cinnamon, soda and salt. In a mixing bowl, cream butter and sugar. Blend in egg and molasses; beat until fluffy. Add the dry ingredients gradually, mixing thoroughly. If desired, chill dough for easier handling. Divide dough into 4 portions. Shape each part into a 15-in. roll on a lightly sugared surface. Flatten to a 15 x 2-1/2-in. strip. Spread 1/4 of the filling down center of each strip. Fold strip in half, lengthwise. Seal edges. Cut into 1-1/2-in. bars. Place on un-greased cookie sheet and bake at 350° for 12 to 15 minutes. Yield: 3 to 4 dozen cookies.

Julie Stauffer, Orrville, Ohio

LEMON CREAM CHEESE MELTS

1/2 cup butter
3 ounces cream cheese
1/2 cup sugar
4 teaspoons lemon peel, grated
2 teaspoons lemon juice

1 cup flour
2 teaspoons baking powder
1/4 teaspoon salt
3/4 cup corn flake crumbs

Cream butter, cheese and sugar until fluffy. Add lemon peel and juice. Stir in flour, baking powder and salt. Chill 1 hour. Drop by teaspoonfuls into corn flake crumbs, roll to coat; shape into balls. Place on ungreased cookie sheet. Bake at 350° 12 to 15 minutes.

Mrs. Jerome Kaltenberg, Arlington, Wisconsin

APPLESAUCE COOKIES

3/4 cup shortening
1 cup brown sugar
1 egg
1/2 cup applesauce
2-1/4 cups flour
1/2 teaspoon baking soda

1/2 teaspoon salt
3/4 teaspoon cinnamon
1/4 teaspoon cloves
1 cup raisins
1/2 cup nuts, chopped

Cream shortening, sugar and egg. Add applesauce, blend well. Combine flour with remaining ingredients. Stir into above mixture. Drop by teaspoonfuls onto greased cookie sheet. Bake at 350° 12 to 15 minutes.

Mrs. Allen Dornbush, Fulton, Illinois

PINEAPPLE-RAISIN DROPS

1 cup brown sugar
1/2 cup butter
1 egg
1 teaspoon vanilla
3/4 cup crushed pineapple, undrained

2 cups flour
1 teaspoon baking powder
1/2 teaspoon baking soda
1/2 teaspoon salt
1/2 cup raisins

Combine sugar, butter, egg and vanilla; beat well. Stir in pineapple. Combine flour, baking powder, soda and salt. Add gradually to creamed mixture, stirring well. Stir in raisins. Drop by teaspoonfuls onto greased cookie sheet. Bake at 375° for 12 to 15 minutes. Yield: 3 dozen.

Lucy Dick, Englevale, North Dakota

HOLIDAY FRUITCAKE COOKIES

4 cups flour
1 teaspoon baking soda
1 teaspoon salt
1 cup butter
2 cups brown sugar
2 eggs, beaten

2/3 cup buttermilk
1 cup pecans, chopped
1 cup candied cherries, chopped
2 cups dates, chopped
1 cup candied fruit
and peels

Combine flour, soda and salt. Cream butter, brown sugar and eggs until light and fluffy. Add buttermilk and flour mixture alternately to creamed mixture. Fold in nuts, cherries, dates and candied fruits. Chill dough. Drop by teaspoonfuls about 2 inches apart onto lightly greased cookie sheets. Top each cookie with red or green cherry half. Bake at 375° 8 to 10 minutes. Remove cookies from baking sheet to wire rack to cool. Yield: 8 dozen.

Marguerite Zoeckler, St. Germain, Wisconsin

LEMON MOONS

2 eggs
2/3 cup vegetable oil
3/4 cup sugar
1/4 cup brown sugar
2 teaspoons grated lemon rind
2 teaspoons lemon juice

2 cups flour
2 teaspoons baking powder
1/2 teaspoon salt
1/4 teaspoon mace
1/4 cup sugar
1/2 teaspoon nutmeg

Combine eggs, oil, sugars, rind and juice. Beat until well blended. Combine flour, baking powder, salt and mace, add to creamed mixture. Drop by teaspoonfuls onto greased cookie sheet. Mix the 1/4 cup sugar and nutmeg in a small bowl. Butter bottom of a glass, dip in sugar-nutmeg mixture and press each cookie flat. Bake at 400° about 8 minutes. Yield: about 4 dozen.

Mrs. Joe Rohlik, Mondovi, Wisconsin

CHERRY PINWHEEL COOKIES

1 cup sugar
1 cup butter
2 eggs, beaten
1/2 teaspoon almond extract

3 cups flour
2 teaspoons baking powder
1/2 teaspoon salt

Cherry Filling:
16-ounce jar maraschino cherries,
    drained, chopped
1 cup cherry liquid

2 tablespoons cornstarch
1/4 teaspoon salt
2 cups ground blanched
    almonds

Cream sugar, butter, eggs and extract until fluffy. Blend in dry ingredients. Chill dough. Roll half of dough into 8 x 12-in. rectangle. Spread with half of cherry filling. Roll up as for jelly roll. Wrap and chill. Repeat with remaining dough. Slice and bake on greased cookie sheet at 375º for 8 to 10 minutes. **Filling:** In saucepan, stir a small amount of cherry liquid into the cornstarch, then add rest of juice. Cook, stirring constantly until thickened. Remove from heat, add salt, chopped cherries and nuts. Cool.

Mrs. Allen I. Hanson, Volin, South Dakota

ORANGE COOKIES

3/4 cup butter or shortening
1-1/2 cup brown sugar
2 eggs
1/2 teaspoon baking soda
1/2 cup buttermilk or sour milk

1/2 cup orange juice
3 cups flour
1 teaspoon salt
1-1/2 teaspoon baking powder

Cream shortening, sugar and eggs. Add soda to milk; add to creamed mixture. Combine dry ingredients, add alternately with juice to creamed mixture. Drop by teaspoonfuls onto greased cookie sheet bake at 350º 8 to 10 minutes. Do not overbake. Note: 1/2 cup chopped nuts may be added to dough. Cookies may be frosted with glaze using confectioners sugar and orange juice. Yield: 3 dozen.

Mrs. Ray Keiper, Palo, Iowa

SPICY APPLE COOKIES

2 cups flour
1 teaspoon baking soda
1/2 teaspoon salt
1-1/2 teaspoon cinnamon
1/2 teaspoon nutmeg
1/2 teaspoon ground cloves
1-1/2 cups apple, chopped
1 cup walnuts, chopped

1 cup raisins
6 ounces butterscotch chips
1-1/4 cup brown sugar
1/2 cup butter
2 eggs
1/4 cup apple juice (milk
    or orange juice)

Combine first six dry ingredients. Combine apple, nuts, raisins and butterscotch chips. Cream butter and sugar, add eggs; beat until fluffy. Stir in apple mixture. Add dry ingredients with juice. Drop by teaspoonfuls onto greased cookie sheet. Bake at 400° 8 to 10 minutes. Remove from cookie sheet while cookie is still warm. Yield: 8 dozen.

Mrs. Harvey Maurer, Reese, Michigan

ANGEL WHISPERS

Filling:
1 egg, beaten
    Grated rind of 1 lemon
4 tablespoons lemon juice

1/2 cup sugar
1 tablespoon butter

Dough:
1/2 cup butter
1/2 cup sugar (may use confectioners)
2 eggs
1/2 teaspoon lemon extract

1/4 teaspoon vanilla
3/4 cup cornstarch
3/4 cup flour
2 teaspoons baking powder

Filling: Combine ingredients and cook until thick. Cool. Cream butter, sugar and eggs until fluffy. Add flavorings. Combine dry ingredients and stir into creamed mixture. Chill dough. Drop by small teaspoonfuls onto cookie sheet, bake at 400° 8 to 10 minutes. Put 2 cookies together with filling. Roll in powdered sugar.

Susan Olson, Sioux Falls, South Dakota

POPPY SEED COOKIES

3/4 cup butter
1-1/3 cup sugar
1/4 cup molasses
1 egg
1 cup pumpkin
1 teaspoon vanilla

2-1/2 cups flour
1 teaspoon baking powder
1 teaspoon baking soda
3/4 cup poppy seed
1 cup pecans, chopped

Mix ingredients in order given. Drop by teaspoonfuls onto greased cookie sheet. Bake at 350° for 10 to 12 minutes. If desired, frost with **Pecan Icing:** 1/4 cup butter, 2 cups confectioners sugar, 1 teaspoon cinnamon, 2 tablespoons molasses, 1/4 cup chopped pecans. Combine ingredients, adding small amount of milk or cream until spreadable.

Mrs. George Hageman, Eldorado, Wisconsin

CHERRY WINKS COOKIES

2-1/4 cups flour
1/2 teaspoon baking soda
1 teaspoon baking powder
1/2 teaspoon salt
3/4 cup shortening
1 cup sugar
2 eggs
2 tablespoons milk

1 teaspoon vanilla
1 cup pecans, chopped
1 cup dates, chopped
1/2 cup maraschino cherries
chopped
2-1/2 cups cornflakes, crushed
Maraschino cherries for
garnish

Combine flour, baking powder, soda and salt. Cream shortening and sugar, blend in egg, milk and vanilla. Stir in dry ingredients, then pecans, dates and chopped cherries. Shape into 1-in. balls, roll in cornflake crumbs, place on greased cookie sheet and top with 1/4 cherry. Bake at 375° for 10 to 12 minutes.

Mrs. Ruth Cox, Quincy, Indiana

MINCEMEAT COOKIES

1-1/2 cup sugar
  1 cup butter
  3 eggs
  1 teaspoon baking soda
  2 tablespoons hot water
  1 teaspoon baking powder

1/2 teaspoon salt
3-1/4 cups flour
1-1/2 cup mincemeat
  1 teaspoon vanilla
  1 cup nuts, chopped

Cream sugar, butter and eggs until fluffy. Dissolve soda in hot water, add to creamed mixture. Combine baking powder, salt and flour, add to creamed mixture alternately with mincemeat. Stir in vanilla and nuts. Drop by teaspoonfuls onto greased cookie sheet. Bake at 375° about 15 minutes.

Mrs. W. N. Peters, Knob Noster, Missouri

CHERRY CHIP COOKIES

3/4 cup shortening (part butter)
  1 cup brown sugar
  1 egg
  1 teaspoon vanilla
2-1/4 cups flour

1 teaspoon baking powder
1/2 teaspoon salt
1/2 cup maraschino cherries, chopped
1/2 cup shredded coconut
6 ounces chocolate chips

Preheat oven to 350°. Cream shortening, sugar, egg and vanilla until light and fluffy. Stir in flour, baking powder and salt. Blend well. Add cherries, coconut and chocolate chips. Drop by teaspoonfuls onto ungreased cookie sheet. Bake for 10 to 12 minutes. Yield: 5 dozen cookies.

Mrs. Leola Guetter, Nevis, Minnesota

DIABETIC RECIPE: *Use unsweetened applesauce to top pancakes, waffles or French toast. So much better than the artificially sweetened syrup.*

Mrs. Harvey H. Witte, Addison, Michigan

Honey Cookies

SCALLOPED HONEY COOKIES

1/2 cup butter
1/2 cup honey
2 cups flour
1 teaspoon baking soda

1/2 teaspoon cinnamon
1/4 teaspoon cloves
1/4 teaspoon allspice
1/4 cup crushed bran flakes

Cream butter and honey. Combine remaining ingredients. Stir into creamed mixture. Roll out dough or drop by teaspoonfuls onto greased cookie sheet, flatten slightly. Bake at 350° 8 to 10 minutes. When cool, frost with 1 cup confectioners sugar, 2 tablespoons honey, 2 teaspoons lemon juice and 1/2 teaspoon grated lemon rind mixed together. Yield: 3 dozen.

Lucy Dick, Englevale, North Dakota

WHOLE WHEAT COOKIES

4 tablespoons butter
1/2 cup honey
1-1/2 cup whole wheat flour
1/4 cup dry milk
1/2 teaspoon baking soda
1/2 teaspoon salt

2 tablespoons water
2 eggs
1/2 teaspoon vanilla
1 cup chocolate chips (6 ounces)
1/2 cup sunflower seeds
1/4 cup chopped peanuts

Combine ingredients in order given. Drop by teaspoonfuls onto lightly greased cookie sheet. Bake at 350° for 12 minutes. Yield: 3 to 4 dozen.

Patrice O'Reilly, Red Wing, Minnesota

SOUR CREAM ANISE COOKIES

1 cup shortening
1 cup brown sugar
3 eggs
1 cup sour cream
1 cup honey

3-1/2 cups flour
3 teaspoons baking soda
1/2 teaspoon anise flavoring
Dash of salt

Cream shortening, sugar; add eggs one at a time, beating well after each addition. Stir in honey, then remaining ingredients, blending well. Drop by teaspoonfuls onto greased cookie sheet. Bake at 350° for 12 to 15 minutes. Remove from cookie sheet and roll in confectioners sugar.

Meleta Schuetzle, Plevna, Montana

SAND BALLS

1 cup butter
1/2 cup confectioners sugar
2 tablespoons honey
2-1/2 cups flour

1/4 teaspoon salt
1 teaspoon vanilla
3/4 cup nuts, chopped

Cream butter, sugar and honey. Add flour, salt, vanilla and nuts. Dough will be stiff. Form into 1-in. balls, chill thoroughly. Place on greased cookie sheet. Bake at 375° about 15 minutes. Roll in confectioners sugar while still warm.

Mrs. Leonard B. Larson, Mabel, Minnesota

BUTTER BEES

1/2 cup butter	1 teaspoon vanilla
1/4 cup honey	1-1/4 cup flour
1 egg	1/4 teaspoon baking powder
1/2 teaspoon maple flavoring	1/4 teaspoon salt

Walnut Filling:

2 tablespoons butter	1 egg yolk
2 tablespoons water	2 teaspoons vanilla
6-1/2 tablespoons honey	1 cup toasted walnuts, chopped

Cream butter, add honey. Beat in egg and flavorings. Blend in dry ingredients. Chill dough. **Walnut filling:** Cook butter, water, honey and egg until thickened. Remove from heat, add nuts and vanilla. Roll dough on floured pastry cloth to 1/8-in. thickness. Cut with 3 round cutters, 1-in., 3/8-in. and 1/2-in. Place large cookie on greased cookie sheet. Spread filling on cookie, top with 3/8-in. cookie; filling, then 1/2-in. cookie. Bake at 375º for 8 to 10 minutes. Cool. Yield: 4 dozen.

Mrs. Alberta Hanson, Cushing, Wisconsin

FIG HONEY COOKIES

3/4 cup sugar	3 teaspoons baking powder
1/2 cup shortening	1/2 teaspoon salt
1/2 cup honey	1 cup figs, chopped
2 eggs	1 cup pecans, chopped
2 tablespoons milk	1 teaspoon lemon extract
2-3/4 cups flour	3 tablespoons orange rind, grated

Cream sugar and shortening. Add honey, well beaten eggs and milk. Combine dry ingredients and stir into creamed mixture. Add remaining ingredients and mix thoroughly. Drop by teaspoonfuls onto well greased cookie sheets. Bake at 425º for 12 minutes. Yield: 3 dozen.

Mrs. Alfred Bayer, Muenster, Texas

NURNBERG LEBKUCHEN

1 cup honey
3/4 cup brown sugar
1 egg
1 tablespoon lemon juice
1 teaspoon lemon rind, grated
2-1/2 cups flour
1/2 teaspoon baking soda

1 teaspoon cinnamon
1/4 teaspoon cloves
1/2 teaspoon allspice
1/2 teaspoon nutmeg
1/2 cup citron, chopped
1/3 cup almonds, chopped
Almond halves and citron
for decoration

Glaze:
1 cup sugar
1/2 cup water

1/4 cup confectioners sugar

Bring honey to a boil, then cool thoroughly. To honey add sugar, beaten egg, lemon rind and juice. Combine flour, soda and spices; stir into honey mixture. Add citron and nuts. Refrigerate overnight. Roll dough 1/2 in. thick. Cut into 2-1/2-in. squares. Place on greased cookie sheet and decorate top with citron and almonds to resemble a flower. Bake at 350° for 10 minutes. Brush with glazing immediately upon removing from oven. **Glaze:** Boil sugar and water until syrup spins a thread from end of spoon. Remove from heat, stir in confectioners sugar. Add couple drops of water and reheat if icing gets too stiff.

Henrietta Seibert, Belleville, Illinois

HONEY COOKIES

1 cup softened butter
1/2 cup honey
1 tablespoon lemon juice
1 egg, separated
1-1/2 teaspoon grated lemon peel

3-1/2 cups flour
1 teaspoon baking powder
1/2 teaspoon salt
1/2 cup nuts, finely chopped

Cream butter and honey. Beat in lemon juice, egg yolk and lemon peel. Stir in dry ingredients. Chill dough. Shape into 1-in. balls, place on greased cookie sheet and flatten with bottom of glass. Brush with slightly beaten egg white, sprinkle with chopped nuts. Bake at 350° for 8 to 10 minutes. Yield: 5 to 6 dozen.

Mrs. Sharon Lee, Black Earth, Wisconsin

Nut Cookies

$100 PECAN ROLL COOKIES

1 cup shortening
1 cup butter
3 cups powdered sugar
1 tablespoon vanilla

3 cups flour
3 cups cornflakes, not crushed
1 cup pecans, ground,
   or finely chopped

Cream shortening and butter (you may use all butter), sugar and vanilla until fluffy. Stir in flour, then corn flakes. Divide dough into 4 portions. Shape into 1-1/2-in. diameter rolls. Roll in ground pecans. Wrap and refrigerate overnight. Slice and bake at 350° about 12 to 15 minutes depending upon thickness of cookie.

Mrs. Raymond W. Erickson, East Grand Forks, Minnesota

GROUND NUT COOKIES

6 egg whites
1 pound confectioners sugar
1 pound ground nuts (any kind)

1/2 cup cracker crumbs
  (soda or graham)
1 teaspoon vanilla

Beat egg whites stiff, but not dry. Add sugar gradually, beating constantly until very stiff. Fold in nuts, crumbs and vanilla. Drop by teaspoonfuls onto greased cookie sheet. Bake at 325° for 8 minutes.

Mrs. Bernhardt Seibert, Belleville, Illinois

FROSTED CASHEW COOKIES

1/2 cup butter
  1 cup brown sugar
  1 egg
1/2 teaspoon vanilla
  2 cups flour

3/4 teaspoon baking powder
3/4 teaspoon baking soda
1/4 teaspoon salt
1/3 cup sour cream
1-3/4 cup salted cashew nuts, broken

Frosting:
1/2 cup butter
  3 tablespoons cream

1/4 teaspoon vanilla
  2 cups confectioners sugar

Cream butter, sugar, egg and vanilla until fluffy. Add combined dry ingredients alternately with sour cream to creamed mixture. Fold in nuts. Drop by teaspoonfuls onto greased cookie sheet. Bake at 400° for 10 minutes. Frost with **Golden Butter Frosting:** Lightly brown butter in saucepan, do not burn. Remove from heat, add cream and vanilla. Stir in sugar, beating until smooth and thick enough to spread. Frost each cookie, top with cashew nut, if desired. Yield: 4-1/2 dozen.

Mrs. Cordella Thompson, Bowman, North Dakota

PECAN CRISPIE COOKIES

1 cup butter
2-1/2 cups brown sugar
2 eggs
2-1/2 cups flour

1/4 teaspoon salt
1/2 teaspoon baking soda
1 cup pecans, chopped

Cream butter and sugar, add eggs one at a time, beating until fluffy. Stir in remaining ingredients. Drop by teaspoonfuls onto greased cookie sheet. Bake at 350° 12 to 15 minutes. Yield: 5 to 6 dozen.

Mrs. Barbara Howard, Pavo, Georgia

SALTED PEANUT CRISPS

1 cup shortening (part butter)
1-1/2 cup brown sugar
2 eggs
2 teaspoons vanilla

3 cups flour
1/2 teaspoon baking soda
1 teaspoon salt
2 cups salted peanuts

Cream shortening, sugar, eggs and vanilla until fluffy. Stir in remaining ingredients. Drop by teaspoonfuls onto greased cookie sheet. Flatten slightly with bottom of glass dipped in sugar. Bake at 375° 8 to 10 minutes. Yield: 6 dozen 2-in. cookies.

Mrs. Dale Hammarlund, Saint Marys, Kansas

ALMOND ROUNDS

3/4 cup butter
1 cup sugar
1/2 teaspoon almond extract
1/2 teaspoon vanilla

1 egg
2 cups flour
1/4 teaspoon salt
1 cup almonds, finely chopped

Cream butter, sugar, flavorings and egg until fluffy. Combine dry ingredients and add to creamed mixture, blending well. Add nuts. Shape into 2-in. roll, wrap and chill. Slice and place on greased cookie sheet. Bake at 350° for about 12 minutes.

Mrs. Wallace Anderson, Colon, Nebraska

Oatmeal Cookies

OATMEAL APPLE-RAISIN COOKIES

2 cups brown sugar
1 cup shortening
4 eggs
1 cup raisins
3/4 cup nuts
1 large apple
3-1/2 cups flour

1 teaspoon cinnamon
1/4 teaspoon salt
1 cup oatmeal
1 teaspoon baking powder
1 teaspoon baking soda
1 teaspoon vanilla

Cream sugar and shortening, add eggs; beat well. Grind raisins, nuts and apple. Add to creamed mixture. Add remaining ingredients, mix well. Drop by teaspoonfuls onto cookie sheet. Bake at 350° until brown, about 12 minutes.

Thelma Bogenhagen, Wallace, Kansas

MOLASSES OATMEAL COOKIES

4-1/4 cups flour
1-1/2 teaspoon salt
  1 tablespoon baking soda
  4 cups oatmeal
1-1/4 cup sugar
1-1/2 teaspoon ginger

1 cup melted shortening
1 cup molasses
2 eggs, beaten
2 tablespoons hot water
1-1/2 cup raisins

Reserve 1/4 cup flour. Combine 4 cups flour, salt and soda. In large bowl combine oatmeal sugar and ginger. Stir in shortening, molasses, eggs, hot water, dry ingredients and raisins. Blend well. Add remaining 1/4 cup flour if needed to roll dough. Roll 1/4-in. thick, cut with cookie cutter. Place on cookie sheet, brush with water and sprinkle with sugar. Bake at 375º 8 to 10 minutes. Note: Dough may be dropped by teaspoonfuls onto greased cookie sheet and baked.

Dorothy V. Karnes, Overbrook, Kansas

LINCOLNSHIRE COOKIES

2-1/2 cups white sugar
  1 cup brown sugar
1-1/2 cup shortening
  3 cups rolled oats
1-1/2 teaspoon salt
  5 cups flour
  2 tablespoons baking powder
1-1/4 teaspoon nutmeg

1 tablespoon cinnamon
2 cups ground raisins
1 cup ground nuts
3 eggs
1/2 cup molasses
1 cup milk
1-1/2 teaspoon baking soda
2 teaspoons vanilla

Mix first 9 ingredients with pastry blender as for pie crust. Add remaining ingredients, mix well. Cover and allow to stand overnight in cool place. Drop by teaspoonfuls onto greased cookie sheet. Flatten with glass. Brush cookie with beaten egg. Bake at 350º for 10 to 12 minutes.

Mrs. Rex O. Fultz, Fort Wayne, Indiana

CHOCOLATE NUT OATMEAL COOKIES

1/2 cup butter
1/2 cup sugar
1/2 cup brown sugar
1 egg, unbeaten
1/3 cup peanut butter
1/2 teaspoon baking soda
1/4 teaspoon salt
1/2 teaspoon vanilla

1 cup flour
1 cup quick oatmeal
1 cup chocolate chips
1/2 cup confectioners sugar
2 to 4 tablespoons evaporated
  milk or cream
1/4 cup peanut butter

Cream butter and sugars. Blend in egg, 1/3 cup peanut butter, soda, salt
and vanilla. Stir in flour, oats and chocolate chips. Drop by teaspoonfuls onto ungreased cookie sheet. Bake at 350° 10 to 15 minutes.
Combine confectioners sugar, milk or cream and peanut butter to make
a glaze. Drizzle over cookies. Yield: 4 dozen.

Julie Rivinius, Littleton, Colorado

OATMEAL ICE BOX COOKIES

1 cup shortening
1 cup white sugar
1 cup brown sugar
2 eggs, well beaten
1 teaspoon vanilla

1-1/2 cup flour
1 teaspoon baking soda
1 teaspoon salt
3 cups quick oatmeal
Chopped peanuts, coconut or raisins

Toast oatmeal in shallow pan in a 300° oven for about 10 minutes.
Cool. Cream shortening and sugars, add eggs and vanilla; beat until
fluffy. Stir in flour, soda and salt; blend well. Note: 1 or 2 teaspoons
cinnamon and 1/2 teaspoon cloves may be added if desired. Fold in
toasted oatmeal. Divide dough into 3 parts. Add one of the above
peanut, coconut, raisins or dates to a portion of the dough for variety.
Form into rolls, wrap and refrigerate overnight. Slice then and bake on
lightly greased cookie sheets. Bake at 350° until browned.

Mrs. Sidney Lorence, Racine, Wisconsin

BANANA DROP COOKIES

3/4 cup shortening
1 cup sugar
1 cup mashed bananas
1 egg
1 teaspoon vanilla
1-1/2 cup flour
1/2 teaspoon baking soda

1 teaspoon baking powder
1/2 teaspoon salt
1/4 teaspoon nutmeg
3/4 teaspoon cinnamon
1 cup oatmeal, uncooked
1/2 cup nuts, chopped

Blend shortening and sugar, stir in banana, egg and vanilla. Combine dry ingredients; stir into creamed mixture. Blend in oatmeal and nuts. Drop by teaspoonfuls onto greased cookie sheet. Bake at 400° about 12 minutes.

Mrs. Erwin Kuehn, Wabasso, Minnesota

COCONUT CRUNCHIES

1 cup butter (part lard
or shortening)
1 cup brown sugar
1 cup white sugar
2 eggs
2 cups flour

2 cups quick oatmeal
2 teaspoons baking soda
1 teaspoon baking powder
1 teaspoon salt
1 teaspoon vanilla
1 cup coconut

Cream butter, sugars and eggs until fluffy. Add remaining ingredients in order given, blending well. Chill dough. Roll into 1-in. balls, place on greased cookie sheet. Bake at 350° 8 to 10 minutes.

Mrs. Harold Voskuil, Sheboygan Falls, Wisconsin

ORANGE OATMEAL COOKIES

1 cup shortening
2 cups brown sugar
2 eggs
2 tablespoons orange rind, grated
1/4 cup orange juice

2 cups flour
1 teaspoon baking soda
3/4 teaspoon salt
2 cups quick oatmeal
1 cup raisins or dates

Cream shortening and sugar, add eggs; beat well. Stir in rind and juice. Add remaining ingredients, mix well. Chill 1 hour or longer. Drop by teaspoonfuls onto greased cookie sheet. Bake at 350° for 12 minutes. Yield: 60 cookies.

Mrs. Sylvia Hester, Salem, Illinois

PEANUT DATE COOKIES

1/2 cup butter
1/2 cup granulated sugar
1 cup brown sugar
1/2 cup chunky peanut butter
3 eggs
1/4 cup water

1 teaspoon vanilla
1 cup flour
1 teaspoon salt
1/2 teaspoon baking soda
3 cups quick oats
1 cup dates, chopped

Cream butter, sugars and peanut butter. Add eggs, water and vanilla, beat until creamy. Add flour, salt and soda, mix until smooth. Add oats and dates. Drop by teaspoonfuls onto greased cookie sheet. Bake at 350° 10 to 12 minutes. Yield: 4 to 5 dozen.

Mrs. F. W. Hoffman, Flintstone, Maryland

OATMEAL BUTTER COOKIES

1 cup soft butter
1 cup confectioners sugar
1-1/2 cup flour

1/2 teaspoon baking soda
1 cup quick oatmeal
2 teaspoons vanilla

Mix in order given. Shape dough into 1-1/2-in. rolls. Roll in chocolate jimmies, pressing them into dough. Chill 2 hours or overnight. Slice, place on ungreased cookie sheet, bake at 325° 12 to 15 minutes.

Mrs. Elsie Rasmussen, Waterbury, Nebraska

TROPICAL OATMEAL COOKIES

1 cup shortening
1 cup sugar
1 cup brown sugar
2 eggs
2-1/2 cups crushed pineapple, undrained
3-1/2 cups quick oatmeal

2 cups flour
1 teaspoon baking soda
1 teaspoon salt
1 teaspoon cinnamon
1/4 teaspoon nutmeg
1 cup walnuts, chopped

Cream shortening and sugars. Beat in eggs, then pineapple. Stir in remaining ingredients in order given. Drop by teaspoonfuls onto ungreased cookie sheet. Bake at 375° 15 minutes.

Julie Rivinius, Littleton, Colorado

GUMDROP COOKIES

1 cup shortening
1 cup brown sugar
1 cup granulated sugar
2 eggs
1 teaspoon vanilla
2 cups flour
1 teaspoon baking powder

1/2 teaspoon baking soda
1/2 teaspoon salt
2 cups quick cooking oats
1 cup coconut
1 cup gumdrops, chopped <u>or</u>
orange slice gumdrop candy,
chopped

Cream shortening, sugars, eggs and vanilla, until fluffy. Combine flour, baking powder, soda and salt. Stir into creamed mixture. Stir in oats, coconut and candy. Drop by teaspoonfuls onto greased cookie sheet. Bake at 375° about 12 minutes.

Mrs. Leonard Celske, Conrath, Wisconsin

NATURAL OATMEAL COOKIES

1/3 cup shortening
1/2 cup brown sugar
1/2 cup granulated sugar
1 egg
1/2 cup raw wheat germ
3/4 cup whole wheat flour
1/2 teaspoon salt

1/2 teaspoon baking powder
1/2 teaspoon baking soda
1/2 teaspoon cloves
1 teaspoon cinnamon
1 cup old-fashion oatmeal
1 cup raisins

Cream shortening and sugars, add egg; blend well. Add wheat germ, flour, salt, baking powder and soda, cloves and cinnamon. Stir until well mixed. Stir in oatmeal and raisins. Shape into walnut size balls, place on ungreased cookie sheet. Bake at 350° 8 to 10 minutes. Cool before removing from cookie sheet. Yield: 3 dozen.

Doris E. Harrison, Naperville, Illinois

Peanut Butter Cookies

PEANUT BUTTER COOKIES

1 cup shortening or margarine
1 cup peanut butter
1 cup white sugar
1 cup brown sugar, firmly packed
2 eggs

3 cups flour
1 teaspoon baking soda
1 teaspoon salt
2 teaspoons vanilla

Cream shortening, peanut butter and sugars. Add eggs one at a time, beating until light and fluffy. Combine flour, soda and salt. Add to creamed mixture, blending well. Add vanilla. Chill dough well for ease in handling. Shape into walnut size balls. Place on greased cookie sheets. Flatten with fork. Bake at 375º for 12 to 15 minutes. Note: For variety, you may add 1 cup chocolate chips or 1 cup salted peanuts, coarsely chopped.

Mrs. Fred Lane, Versailles, Kentucky

SCOTCH KRISPIES

1/2 cup butter
1/2 cup peanut butter
1/2 cup sugar granulated
1/2 cup brown sugar
1 egg
1/2 teaspoon vanilla

1 cup flour
1/2 teaspoon baking soda
1/4 teaspoon baking powder
1/4 teaspoon salt
2 cups Rice Krispies cereal
6 ounces butterscotch chips

Cream butter, peanut butter and sugars. Add egg and vanilla, beat well. Stir in flour, soda, baking powder and salt. Add cereal and butterscotch chips. Drop by teaspoonfuls onto greased cookie sheet. Bake at 375º 10 to 15 minutes.

Mrs. Joan Luchritz, Clinton, Iowa

EASY PEANUT BUTTER COOKIES

1 cup peanut butter
1 cup sugar

1 egg

Preheat oven to 325º. Cream sugar and egg, add peanut butter. Roll into balls about the size of a walnut. Place on lightly greased cookie sheet, flatten with fork; bake for 15 minutes. Yield: 3 dozen.

Nina J. Bowles, Southside, West Virginia

MAGIC 6-WAY COOKIE RECIPE

1-1/3 cup Eagle brand
      sweetened condensed milk

1/2 cup smooth peanut butter

ONE of the following:
2 cups white raisins
2 cups corn flakes
3 cups shredded coconut

2 cups bran flakes
1 cup nuts, chopped
2 cups dates, chopped

Mix milk with peanut butter. Add *one* of the above listed ingredients. Drop by teaspoonfuls onto well greased cookie sheet. Bake at 375º for 12 minutes. Remove from pan at once.

Mrs. Jesse Warner, Utica, Ohio

PEANUT BUTTER PINWHEELS

1/2 cup shortening
1 cup sugar
1/2 cup peanut butter
1 egg
2 tablespoons milk

1-1/4 cup flour
1/2 teaspoon salt
1/2 teaspoon baking soda
6 ounces chocolate chips

Cream shortening and sugar. Beat in peanut butter, egg and milk. Stir in the flour, salt and soda. Chill dough for about 1/2 hour for ease in handling. Roll dough on a floured board or between 2 sheets of waxed paper to a rectangle 13 x 8 x 1/4 in. Melt chocolate chips, cool slightly. Spread over dough. Roll as for jelly roll. Chill for 1/2 hour (no longer or chocolate will harden and crack as you slice cookies). Slice 1/4 in. thick; place on ungreased cookie sheets and bake at 375° for 8 to 10 minutes. Yield: 4 dozen.

Mrs. Gene Wirth, New Raymer, Colorado

PEANUT BLOSSOMS

1-3/4 cup flour
1 teaspoon baking soda
1/2 teaspoon salt
1/2 cup shortening
1/2 cup peanut butter

1/2 cup sugar
1/2 cup brown sugar
1 egg
1 teaspoon vanilla
Milk chocolate candy kisses

Preheat oven to 350°. Combine flour, soda and salt. Cream shortening, peanut butter, sugars and egg until light and fluffy. Add vanilla. Add dry ingredients and blend well. Shape dough into 1-1/2-in. balls, roll in granulated sugar; place on greased cookie sheets. Bake for 10 to 12 minutes. Remove from oven. Top each cookie with a candy kiss, pressing down firmly so cookie cracks around edge. Return to oven; bake 3 minutes longer. Yield: 3 dozen.

Mrs. Bill Graham, Powell, Wyoming

PEANUT BUTTER SANDWICH COOKIES

1-1/2 cup flour
  1/2 cup sugar
  1/2 teaspoon baking soda
  1/4 teaspoon salt
  1/2 cup shortening

1/2 cup peanut butter
1/4 cup light corn syrup
  1 tablespoon milk
    Peanut butter

In bowl, combine flour, sugar, soda and salt. Cut in shortening and peanut butter until mixture resembles coarse meal. Blend in syrup and milk. Shape into roll about 2 in. in diameter. Wrap and chill. Slice 1/8 in. thick. Place half the slices on ungreased cookie sheet. Spread each cookie with 1/2 teaspoon peanut butter. Cover with remaining slices. Seal edges with tines of fork. Bake at 350º for 10 to 12 minutes. Cool slightly. Remove from cookie sheet to wire rack. Yield: 2-1/2 dozen.

Mrs. Stanley Voorhees, Jr., Hudson, New York

PEANUT BUTTERSCOTCH COOKIES

1/2 cup shortening
1/2 cup brown sugar
1/4 cup white sugar
  2 eggs
1/2 teaspoon vanilla
1/2 cup peanut butter

1 cup flour
1 teaspoon baking soda
1/4 teaspoon salt
1/2 cup quick oats
  1 cup butterscotch chips (6-oz.)

Cream shortening, sugars, eggs and vanilla until fluffy. Stir in peanut butter, then flour, soda and salt. Blend in oats and chips. Roll into balls the size of a walnut. Bake at 350º for 10 to 12 minutes. Yield: 3 dozen.

Mrs. Carol Thomas, Enid, Oklahoma

KID-SIZE COOKIES: *Use the top of coffee pot as a cookie cutter. Makes giant cookies kids love.*

Mrs. Sallie Bristow, Mattoon, Illinois

Raisin-Date Cookies

AUNT EMMA'S COOKIES

2 cups dates, chopped	2 teaspoons cinnamon
2 cups raisins	1 teaspoon cloves
1/2 cup nuts, chopped	1/2 teaspoon salt
1 cup water	2 teaspoons baking soda
3 cups brown sugar	6 cups flour
1 cup shortening	1/2 cup milk
4 eggs	

Combine first 4 ingredients and cook together 5 minutes, cool. Cream shortening and sugar, add eggs one at a time; beat until fluffy. Combine dry ingredients and add alternately with milk to creamed mixture. Add fruit-nut mixture. Drop by teaspoonfuls onto greased cookie sheet. Bake at 375° for 15 minutes. Yield: 8 dozen.

Mrs. Carolynne M. Wanner, Coatesville, Pennsylvania

RITZ DATE COOKIES

1/2 pound dates, chopped
  1 can Bordens Eagle brand
    sweetened condensed milk

1 cup nuts, chopped
Ritz crackers
Frosting

Cook dates and condensed milk until thick, stirring constantly. Add nuts. When cool, top each cracker with 1 teaspoon date mixture. Bake at 350° for 7 minutes. **Frosting:** Brown 3 tablespoons butter, add 3 tablespoons cream. Stir in enough confectioners sugar to make frosting spreadable.

Mrs. Walter Peck, Rochester, Minnesota

FRY PAN COOKIES

1/2 cup butter
  1 cup sugar
  1 cup dates, chopped
  1 egg, beaten

2 cups Rice Krispie cereal
1/2 cup nuts, chopped
1 teaspoon vanilla
Coconut

Combine butter, sugar, dates and egg in saucepan. Melt slowly and simmer for 5 minutes, stirring constantly. Remove from heat, add cereal, nuts and vanilla. Roll into balls then into coconut.

Jo Ann Westervelt, Lodi, New York

ROSY RAISIN PECAN COOKIES

2 cups flour
1 cup sugar
1 teaspoon baking powder
1/2 teaspoon baking soda
2 teaspoons allspice
1 teaspoon cinnamon

1/2 teaspoon ground cloves
1 cup shortening
2 eggs
1 can condensed tomato soup
2 cups raisins
1 cup pecans, chopped

Combine dry ingredients. Add shortening, eggs and soup. Beat at medium speed for 2 minutes. Fold in raisins and nuts. Drop by teaspoonfuls onto ungreased cookie sheet. Bake at 350° for 8 to 10 minutes.

Mrs. Otto Stank, Pound, Wisconsin

RAISIN FILLED BROWN SUGAR COOKIES

Filling:

1 cup raisins, chopped
1 cup brown sugar

1 tablespoon flour
1 cup water

Dough:

2 cups brown sugar
1 cup shortening
2 eggs, lightly beaten
  Dash salt

1 teaspoon baking soda,
  dissolved in 1 teaspoon
  hot water
4 cups flour (scant)

Boil filling ingredients until thick. Set aside to cool. Cream sugar, shortening, eggs and salt until fluffy. Add soda and flour. Roll dough thin. Cut into circles or squares. Place a scant teaspoonful of filling on each cookie. Cover with another cookie. Seal edges. Place on cookie sheet and bake at 400° for 8 to 10 minutes.

Mrs. George Ott, Reeder, North Dakota

MOIST RAISIN COOKIES

1-1/2 cup sugar
1/2 cup butter
2 eggs, beaten
3 cups flour
1-1/2 teaspoon baking soda
1/2 teaspoon cinnamon
1/2 teaspoon cloves

1/2 teaspoon nutmeg
1 cup raisins
1-1/4 cup water
2/3 cup water from
  cooked raisins (hot)
1/2 teaspoon salt
1/2 cup nuts, chopped

Cream sugar and butter, add eggs and beat well. Combine flour, soda and spices; add to creamed mixture. Cook raisins in 1-1/4 cup water, drain. Add raisins to batter and 2/3 cup of hot raisin water. Mix well. Drop by teaspoonfuls onto greased cookie sheet. Bake at 350° for 10 to 12 minutes.

Mrs. Carol Hinkle, Sedalia, Missouri

FILLED APPLE DATE COOKIES

Filling:

1-1/2 cup apples, chopped
1 cup dates, chopped
3 tablespoons sugar

1/4 teaspoon cinnamon
2 tablespoons orange juice
1 teaspoon lemon juice

Dough:

1/2 cup shortening
1 cup brown sugar
1 egg
1/4 cup milk

3 cups flour
2 teaspoons baking powder
1/2 teaspoon salt
1 teaspoon vanilla

Filling: Combine ingredients and cook until thick, cool. Cream shortening and sugar, add egg; beat well. Blend in milk. Stir in flour, baking powder and salt. Add vanilla. Chill dough for 2 hours. Roll out on lightly floured board. Cut into 2-in. squares. Place 1 tablespoon filling on each square. Top with another square and seal with fork. Bake on greased cookie sheet at 350° until browned.

Mrs. Allen J. Dornbush, Fulton, Illinois

DATE PINWHEEL COOKIES

1 pound dates, chopped
1/2 cup orange juice
1 cup walnuts, finely chopped
1/2 cup sugar
1 cup shortening
1 cup granulated sugar

1 cup brown sugar
3 eggs, well beaten
1 teaspoon vanilla
4 cups flour
1-1/2 teaspoon baking soda
1 teaspoon salt

Combine date, juice, walnuts and 1/2 cup sugar, cook 10 minutes, stirring frequently. Set aside to cool. Cream shortening, sugars and eggs until light and fluffy. Combine flour, soda and salt; stir into creamed mixture. Chill dough if necessary for ease in rolling. Roll to 1/4-in. thickness, spread with filling. Roll jelly roll fashion and chill overnight. Slice 1/8 in. thick and bake at 375° for 10-12 minutes.

Mrs. Ernest Bartels, Peshtigo, Wisconsin

DATE COCONUT COOKIES

1-1/2 cup sugar
   2 eggs, beaten
1-1/2 cup coconut
   1 cup dates, chopped
   1 teaspoon vanilla

1 cup dairy sour cream
3 cups flour
3 teaspoons baking powder
1/2 teaspoon baking soda
1 teaspoon salt

Combine sugar and eggs, beat well. Add coconut, dates and vanilla.
Blend well. Combine dry ingredients, add alternately with sour cream
to creamed mixture. Drop by teaspoonfuls onto greased cookie sheets
and bake at 350° for 10 to 12 minutes.

Mrs. Wm. Ashley, St. Johns, Michigan

DELECTABLE DATE DROPS

   1 cup dates, chopped
1/2 cup water
   1 egg
1/2 cup brown sugar
1/2 cup butter
1/4 cup milk

1-1/2 cup flour
1/2 teaspoon salt
1/2 teaspoon baking powder
1/4 teaspoon baking soda
1/2 cup nuts, chopped

Combine dates and water, bring to boil; simmer 5 minutes. Set aside to
cool. Reserve 2 tablespoons for frosting. Into remaining date mixture,
beat in egg, sugar, butter and milk. Combine flour, salt, baking powder
and soda. Add to date mixture. Fold in nuts. Drop by teaspoonfuls
onto ungreased cookie sheet. Bake at 350° for 10 to 12 minuts. Cool.
Frost with date frosting made with 3 tablespoons butter, 1-1/2 cup
confectioners sugar, 1/2 teaspoon vanilla and the reserved 2 tablespoons
date mixture. Add enough milk to make spreadable. Yield: 3 dozen.

Mrs. Otto Stank, Pound, Wisconsin

Spice-Molasses Cookies

LACE COOKIES

1 cup flour
1 teaspoon cinnamon
Dash nutmeg
1/4 teaspoon salt
1/2 teaspoon baking soda

3/4 teaspoon baking powder
1/2 cup butter
1/2 cup sugar
1/2 cup sorghum or light molasses
1 teaspoon lemon extract

Combine flour, spices, salt, soda and baking powder. Melt butter with sugar and molasses over boiling water. Remove from heat, add dry ingredients and lemon extract, beat until smooth. Let stand over hot water 5 minutes. Drop by teaspoonfuls onto greased cookie sheet, 3-in. apart. Bake at 325° for 10 minutes. Allow to cool 2 or 3 minutes before removing from sheet. Shape into roll or cone.

Mrs. Gerhardt Kiekhaefer, Greenleaf, Wisconsin

OLD-FASHIONED DARK COOKIES

1 cup brown sugar
1 cup shortening
1 egg
1/2 teaspoon salt
1/4 cup dark molasses
1/2 cup maple syrup

1 teaspoon baking soda
1 teaspoon cinnamon
1 teaspoon nutmeg
1/2 cup warm water
2-1/2 cups flour

Cream sugar and shortening. Add egg, salt, molasses, syrup soda, spices and warm water. Stir in flour. Drop by teaspoonfuls onto greased cookie sheet. Bake at 350° about 10 minutes.

Mrs. Harold C. Magnussen, Milton, Vermont

SANTA CLAUS COOKIES

3/4 cup butter
3/4 cup shortening
1/4 teaspoon nutmeg
1 tablespoon cinnamon
1/2 teaspoon cloves
3/4 teaspoon baking soda

1 cup brown sugar
1 cup white sugar
3-1/4 cups flour
4 tablespoons light cream
3/4 cup sliced almonds

Cream butter and shortening. Combine dry ingredients and stir into creamed butter. Blend in cream. Stir in nuts. Form into 2 rolls, wrap and refrigerate overnight. Slice thin and bake on ungreased cookie sheets at 350° for 10 to 15 minutes.

Mrs. Albert Nywening, Goshen, New York

MOLASSES CRINKLES

3/4 cup shortening
1 cup brown sugar
1 egg
1/4 cup molasses
2-1/4 cups flour

2 teaspoons soda
1/4 teaspoon salt
1/2 teaspoon cloves
1 teaspoon cinnamon
1 teaspoon ginger

Cream shortening, sugar, egg and molasses. Combine dry ingredients and stir into creamed mixture. Chill dough. Roll into balls the size of a walnut. Dip tops in sugar. Place sugar side up on greased baking sheet. Sprinkle each cookie with 2 or 3 drops of water to produce a crackled surface. Bake at 350° for 10 to 12 minutes. Yield: 4 dozen.

Mrs. Otto Stank, Pound, Wisconsin

PEPPER NUTS

1 cup sour cream
2 cups butter
4 eggs
3 cups brown sugar
1 teaspoon cinnamon
1 teaspoon ginger
1 teaspoon nutmeg

1 teaspoon cloves
1 teaspoon black pepper
1 teaspoon baking powder
1 teaspoon baking soda
1/2 teaspoon salt
8 to 10 cups flour
1 cup nuts, chopped fine

Cream sour cream, butter, eggs and sugar until fluffy. Combine flour (I use 8-1/2 cups) spices and remaining dry ingredients. Add to creamed mixture to form a stiff dough. Add nuts. Chill dough. Roll in penny size rolls, chill. Slice thin. Bake at 375° for 10 minutes or until brown and crisp.

Mrs. Carolyn Henard, Plains, Texas

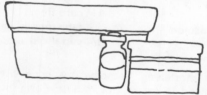

NUTMEG LOGS

1 cup butter, softened
2 teaspoons vanilla
2 teaspoons rum flavoring
3/4 cup sugar

1 egg
3 cups flour
1/4 teaspoon salt
1 teaspoon nutmeg

Preheat oven to 350°. Cream butter with flavorings, sugar and egg until fluffy. Combine flour, salt and nutmeg; add to creamed mixture, blend well. Shape pieces of dough into long rolls, 1/2-in. in diameter on a sugared board. Cut in 3-in. lengths, place on greased cookie sheet and bake for 12 to 15 minutes. Cool and frost with icing. Mark icing with tines of fork to resemble bark. Yield: 72 cookies. **Icing:** 1/3 cup butter, 1 teaspoon vanilla, 2 teaspoons rum flavoring, 2 cups confectioners sugar and 2 tablespoons light cream. Combine ingredients; beat until creamy.

Mrs. Anna LaBarr, Penn Yan, New York

CRY BABY COOKIES

1 cup sugar
1/2 cup butter
1/2 cup shortening
2 eggs
1/2 cup molasses
1 tablespoon vinegar
1 cup strong hot coffee

2 teaspoons baking soda
2 cups raisins
4 cups flour
2 teaspoons cinnamon
1 teaspoon ginger
1/2 teaspoon salt

Pour coffee over raisins and soda, set aside. Cream sugar, butter, shortening and eggs until light and fluffy. Add vinegar and molasses. Combine flour and spices, add alternately with coffee-raisin mixture. Drop by teaspoonfuls onto cookie sheet. Bake at 375° 9 to 10 minutes.

Mrs. N. Travland, Coronach, Sask., Canada

COOL COOKIES: *To keep drop cookies from spreading while baking, chill the dough for several hours. Drop by teaspoonfuls 2-in. apart onto cookie sheet.*

Mrs. A. Mancheski, Valders, Wisconsin

QUICK COOKIE FROSTING: *Snip off the plastic top of a catsup dispenser. Fill with frosting and squeeze frost or decorate cookies.*

Mrs. Gene Pester, Hingham, Montana

SUGAR SHAKER: *Mix dry, flavored gelatin and equal amount of sugar in a salt shaker. Use this mixture to top your next batch of sugar cookies. The gelatin adds an interesting flavor and color.*

Mrs. Ed Johnson, Clarkston, Washington

Assortment of Cookies

CREAM WAFERS

1 cup soft butter
1/3 cup whipping cream

2 cups flour

Mix ingredients, chill thoroughly. Roll 1/8-in. thick and cut in 1-1/2-in. rounds. Place on waxed paper, heavily sprinkled with granulated sugar. Turn to coat both sides of cookie. Place on baking sheet, prick tops in 3 or 4 places with fork. Bake at 375° about 8 minutes. Cool. Put together with **Creamy Frosting:** 1/4 cup butter, 3/4 cup confectioners sugar, 1 egg yolk and 1 teaspoon vanilla *or* almond extract. Tint frosting if desired. Note: You may roll pieces of this dough the size of a pencil about 6-in. long. Shape into a pretzel and bake as above.

Mrs. Darrell W. Reed, Spragueville, Iowa

BUTTERHORN COOKIES

4 cups flour
1/2 cup sugar
1/2 teaspoon salt
1 package dry yeast

1-1/4 cup butter
1/2 cup sour cream
6 egg yolks
1 teaspoon vanilla

Nut Filling:
6 egg whites
1-1/2 cup sugar
1 teaspoon vanilla

1 teaspoon cinnamon
2 cups nuts, chopped

Combine flour, sugar, salt and yeast. Cut in butter as for pie crust. Combine sour cream, yolks and vanilla; add to above mixture and blend well. Shape into ball and refrigerate about 2 hours. Divide dough into 4 portions, work with one portion, keep rest of dough refrigerated. Roll into 9 or 10-in. circles. Cut into 12 wedges, drop a large spoonful of Nut Filling on each wedge. Roll wedge into butterhorn and arrange on greased cookie sheet. Bake at 325° for about 30 minutes, until lightly browned. Yield: 8 dozen. **Nut Filling:** Beat egg whites until soft peaks form. Gradually add 1-1/2 cup sugar, beating until stiff and glossy. Fold in cinnamon and nuts. Note: Although recipe contains yeast, you do not allow dough to rise before baking. Horns may be glazed with butter icing, if desired.

Mrs. Lauraine Smolik, Judson, Indiana

KISSES

5 egg whites
1/2 teaspoon cream of tartar
1/2 teaspoon salt
1/2 cup brown sugar
1 cup white sugar

1/2 teaspoon vanilla
1 cup nuts, chopped
1/2 cup dates, chopped, optional
1/2 cup chocolate chips, optional

Beat egg whites until frothy, add cream of tartar and salt; beat in sugar a few tablespoonfuls at a time, continuing to beat until meringue is stiff and glossy. Fold in vanilla, nuts and one of the optional ingredients, or some of each, depending upon your taste. Bake at 275° 40 to 45 minutes.

Mrs. Wayne Heindel, Celina, Ohio

POTATO CHIP BUTTERSCOTCH COOKIES

1 cup butter
1 cup white sugar
1 cup brown sugar
2 eggs
1 teaspoon vanilla
2 cups flour
1 teaspoon baking soda

2 cups coarsely crushed potato
chips
1 cup butterscotch chips
(6-ounces)
1/2 cup nuts, chopped, optional
Chocolate star candies, optional

Cream butter, sugars, eggs and vanilla until fluffy. Stir in potato chips
and butterscotch chips, then flour and soda. Roll into balls, or drop by
teaspoonfuls onto cookie sheet, flatten slightly. Bake at 350° for 10 to
12 minutes. Top with chocolate star, if desired.

Florence Proctor, Elkhorn, Wisconsin

GOLDEN CARROT COOKIES

3/4 cup shortening
3/4 cup sugar
1 cup grated raw carrots
1 teaspoon vanilla

1 egg, beaten
2 cups flour
1/2 teaspoon salt
2 teaspoons baking powder

Cream shortening and sugar, add carrots, vanilla and egg. Stir in
remaining ingredients. Drop by teaspoonfuls onto greased cookie sheet.
Bake at 375° about 12 minutes.

Mrs. Gary Holladay, Lawrence, Kansas

BREAKFAST YEAST COOKIES

2 packages dry yeast
2/3 cup warm water
1-1/2 cup butter, softened
3 cups flour

1/2 teaspoon salt
1 cup quick oats
1 cup flaked coconut
1/2 cup sugar

Dissolve yeast in warm water. Mix butter into flour and salt until
crumbly. Stir in oats and coconut. Add yeast, blend well. Chill dough at
least 1 hour, or overnight. To bake, hand roll dough into walnut size
balls. Roll in the 1/2 cup sugar, place on lightly greased cookie sheet,
flatten slightly and make an indentation in center of cookie with
thumb. Fill center with jam, jelly or a nutmeat. Bake at 350° for 15
minutes. Yield: 60 cookies.

Mrs. Irene Johnson, Cedar Falls, Iowa

POPPY SEED COOKIES

1 cup butter	1/2 teaspoon vanilla
1 cup sugar	1/2 teaspoon almond extract
2 eggs	1/4 teaspoon salt
1-1/2 teaspoon baking powder	3 cups flour
1/2 cup poppy seed	Cinnamon and sugar

Combine all ingredients and beat with electric mixer. Dough will be stiff. Divide dough into 3 portions. Shape into 3 rolls. Wrap and refrigerate. Slice, place on greased cookie sheet, sprinkle with cinnamon and sugar. Bake at 350° for 10 minutes.

Mrs. Harold Schuette, North Freedom, Wisconsin

CORN MEAL COOKIES

1 cup shortening	1 teaspoon baking powder
1-1/2 cup sugar	1/2 teaspoon salt
2 eggs	1 teaspoon nutmeg
1 teaspoon lemon extract	1 cup white or yellow corn meal
3 cups flour	1/2 cup white raisins

Cream sugar and shortening, add eggs one at a time, beating well after each addition; add extract. Combine dry ingredients, add to creamed mixture. Stir in raisins. Shape into a roll 1-1/2-in. in diameter. Wrap and chill at least 2 hours or overnight. Slice and bake at 350° for 10 minutes.

Mrs. Lynn Herrick, Delta, Iowa

DOUGHNUT SHAPED COOKIES: *Use the doughnut cutter for rolled cookies for the children. Hole in the center is great for little tots to hold.*

Mrs. Clara Hill, Langdon, North Dakota

Index

Plenty More Tasty Recipes

PEANUT BUTTER FAVORITES. If peanut butter is your favorite...this cookbook is for you! Peanut Butter Favorites offers more than 150 of the best "nutty" array of new desserts and snacks, but also scrumptious salads, peanutty side dishes and protein-rich main dishes. This book will surely get a stamp of approval from your entire family. (0215) $3.95.

BAR COOKIE BONANZA. Quick, delicious, pretty and practical. Those four words describe the bar cookie recipes in this cookbook, all of them gathered from readers of Country Extra. What's best, most of these bars are a snap to make—you'll find you can put them together and bake them nearly as fast as they'll disappear! (0205) $3.95.

MY, OH MY, COUNTRY PIES. Who could help but exclaim, "My, oh my" when trying to select which of these country pies to make first! This book contains more than 120 exciting, innovative pie recipes of all kinds. Whip up one of these taste-tempting pies to surprise your family for no special reason! (0212) $3.95.

COUNTRY SQUASH. This cookbook will show you how to prepare prolific squash in more than 130 enticing ways. This book includes casseroles and quiches, cookies and cakes. It tells you how to make squash something more than a simple side dish. Those of you who grow zucchini will especially enjoy the chapter devoted to unique zucchini ideas. (0214) $3.95.

RECIPES FOR LEFTOVERS. Here's a cookbook filled with great ideas that answer that frequent question, "What should I do with all these leftovers?" The book is divided into convenient sections, giving recipes for leftover beef, pork, poultry, vegetables, etc. (0016) $3.95.

TAKE 3 AND SAVE $2.90! Order any combination of three cookbooks and you pay only $8.95! Just list the titles and quantity of each (include Code Numbers, please) and enclose $8.95 plus $1.25 postage/handling.

To order an extra copy of Cookie Jar Cookbook (0153) or any of these cookbooks, just send $3.95, plus 75¢ for postage and handling, to Country Store, Suite 993, Box 572, Milwaukee WI 53201. For orders or more than one book, please include 75¢ for postage/handling for the first book and 25¢ more for each additional book.